The Cage Was
Her Cocoon

The Cage Was Her Cocoon:

A Journey from Prison Administrator to Entrepreneur

Constantine J. Alleyne

ISBN: 978-0-578-76335-4

Dedicated to the brave men and women who work behind the wall with little to no recognition for their sacrifice, the impact that you have on the industry, and on the lives of the offenders and their families.
Know that there is power in your experience.
Your voice IS big enough!

And

To my family, who have supported me through all of life's challenges and victories. Words cannot express my gratitude for your encouragement and continuous prayers.
I love you all.

Table of Contents

Conclusion

FOREWORD

I was extremely lucky the day a good friend of mine introduced me to Constantine Alleyne. At the time, I was looking for someone who would be willing to come onto my YouTube channel and talk about the non-uniform side of working in Corrections. I was looking to balance my custody experience with someone, with a solid correctional comprehension, who could represent working on the civilian's side of prisons and jails. It was only supposed to be for one show, but instead, Connie has become an integral part of the Tier Talk family.

The Cage Was Her Cocoon, is a journey into the heart and soul of humanity. Connie has a level of strength that is founded in her ability to be vulnerable. It's a rare gift that can only be discovered by someone who has the courage to go deep within themselves. As detailed in her book, it's a road defined by determination, self-discovery, and transformation.

Each page is a connection to a world that provides the reader with hope. Hope is such a needed element in today's world. Hope is a promise that tomorrow can be better if we just get through today. And, for me, reading *The Cage Was Her Cocoon* is the PROMISE that we all need right now.

As a colleague and friend of Connie's, I am honored to be given this opportunity to write a foreword for her book. It is so humbling to know, out of all the people she could have chosen, she chose me. I felt like I was finally picked first in gym class! Having this opportunity is a true gift for me that adds so much value to my existence and purpose. I have learned so much from the expertise Connie brings to the Tier Talk family and from reading The Cage Was Her Cocoon, which adds a deeper level of connection.

Very few of us get to see the inside of a cocoon during the transition from a caterpillar to a butterfly. Connie has taken us inside the cocoon, and she is showing us, first-hand, both the struggle and the promise of better days to come.

Anthony Gangi,
Host, Tier Talk and Correctional Advocate

INTRODUCTION

"My philosophy is that not only are you responsible for your life but doing the best at this moment puts you in the best place for the next moment."

–OPRAH WINFREY

"BREAK FREE! BREAK FREE! BREAK FREE!" You may be wondering, "From what?" Well, I'd like to invite you on a short journey with me. Would you mind taking a moment to reflect on your life? Specifically, I'd like to draw your attention to that job that was once the best thing that ever happened to you. Does it still bring you satisfaction? Consider that friendship that you know you've outgrown. Perhaps you were once excited about your marriage but now you find yourself indifferent. Are you still trying hard to live up to your family's expectations? I believe we can agree that this is not a fulfilling state of existence and it cannot be sustained. Eventually, you will not only want to but need to break free.

Those are the exact experiences I would like to call your attention to. Perhaps you've learned how to live with them. You have made the necessary adjustments to suppress those unsettling feelings; however, suppressing them is unhealthy. Actually, suppressing them is depriving you from living the life you always imagined for yourself. See, these are the experiences I refer to as "cage experiences." A cage experience is any experience or situation that holds you captive, making you feel stuck or even trapped. For some, the cage may be an actual place, like a prison or jail. For others, the cage may be a job or a situation that is holding them mentally hostage because they cannot see their way out.

Do you know what I'm talking about?

Like the cocoon for a butterfly, those cage experiences are where the transformation occurs—all the growth and development needed to completely change your state of existence. But unlike the caterpillar, we have a choice. We can choose to surrender what we are for what we could become. We can choose to extract the value from our cages and leave behind what no longer supports us in becoming the best versions of ourselves.

We can choose to extract the value from our cages and leave behind what no longer supports us in becoming the best versions of ourselves.

Let me add a little context to our journey. Merriam Webster defines a cage "as a box or enclosure having some openwork for confining or carrying animals (such as birds)." You, my friend, are no animal. However, there may be people, places, and/or situations that confine you. Do they carry you through your life decisions? They may even be the driving force behind your actions or inactions.

You may be thinking ... this book is too real; this is speaking to my exact situation right now. Do you have your cage experience(s) in mind? I don't know about you, but I've had many cage experiences in my lifetime. In fact, I worked in an actual cage—jails, and prisons—for almost two decades. Admittedly, my cage taught me a great deal about myself, about the profession, and most importantly about life.

The cage feels uncomfortable once you start to grow, just as the experience of the caterpillar transforming into the chrysalis. It may even hurt when you start trying to pry those bars open, but you can see your purpose, so you can't stop trying despite how painful it is.

I get it, you do not want to live your life as a caterpillar when you know there is something so amazing in your DNA—in your future. To reach your life's fullest potential, you cannot remain complacent in your comfort zone.

President Barack Obama once said, "Change is never easy, but always possible."

That cage, your comfort zone, is the place you created to make your cage experience easy, more tolerable. It makes me think of that statement: "Whatever helps you sleep at night!"

I would like to think that I was always the master of my universe but there's been external forces that influenced my decisions to stay or go. Unfortunately, we are quite effective and efficient at confining ourselves in difficult situations for the unconscious purpose of living our life through that familiar, painful cage. As I look deeper into our natural propensity to lie stagnant, the closest thing I can relate this cage experience to is the term "inner passivity."

According to Dr. Dan Green, inner passivity is defined as an unconscious emotional element that limits the flow of our creativity or hinders our self-expression. It refers to the "manner in which we hold on to negative emotions and create our own self-misery and doubt." Inner passivity is often experienced as a lack of inertia or as a lack of foresight or vision. It is also the inclination to view what you are actively doing as if it were being done to you, without your consent.

Please let this serve as a gentle reminder that things aren't just happening to you. You have the power to shift gears and to act. Unlike matters relative to your genetic material, like Type I Diabetes, for example, you *can* hurdle those circumstances you may have been born into. You *can* take control of your life and create the future you desire. No one is saying that this mindset shift, nor the accompanying work will be easy, what I am saying is that it is possible.

The Cage Was Her Cocoon provides a four-step guide to getting you from struggle to strength.

Step I: Adjust **your** depth of focus

Step II: Create mental distance

Step III: Tap into your social intelligence

Step IV: Create a plan

Each cage experience will reveal something new to you. My cages gave me clarity and more information to make better decisions for myself and cultivated the discipline I needed to get through the challenging times.

Some of my cage experiences lasted longer than others and that's ok because it reflected the time *I* needed to glean the lessons that were meant for *me*. If you are in the midst of a cage experience, understand that you have the power to shift gears and change direction. Together, we will explore the manner in which I consistently experienced my cages:

* Phase I: Acknowledgement

* Phase II: Discovery

* Phase III: Heavy Lifting

* Phase IV: Victory

Know that your worth surpasses what your mind can conceive. So let's work through this together.

The Cage Was Her Cocoon provides practical recom-

mendations to achieve
the mental transfor- **Know that your worth**
mation required to **surpasses what your**
free yourself and move **mind can conceive.**
to the next phase of
your life: getting you closer to fulfilling your life's
purpose. The cage you find yourself in today is developing the strength you need for tomorrow.

Phase I: Acknowledgement

Chapter 1

A Cage of Comfort

"Comfort is your biggest trap and coming out of comfort zone your biggest challenge."
— Manoj Arora

This is one of the most common cages because it is where we feel most comfortable. We have made it nice and cozy here. It is your comfort zone; it's where everything is familiar. It requires you to do no ***heavy lifting***. It is where you feel most in control and where you can predict what will happen next.

My friends, family, and home are my comfort zone. That's where I let my hair down and where I am most vulnerable. I recently received a text message from StacyAnn, one of my closest friends. The text read, "Watch whenever you feel doubtful. You got this!" It was just what I needed when I needed it. Because I was feeling doubtful, I decided to watch, *She Did That* on Netflix.

I started my entrepreneurial journey in 2018. This very friend and I were having a glass of wine on a Friday night talking about how we were going to take over the world, LOL! As our daughters were running up and down the stairs hounding us about when the pizza delivery was going to arrive, StacyAnn said to me, "Connie, you have way too much experience and goodness going on for you to not do anything with it."

As many women do, I said, "Girl, nobody wants to hear me talk about my experiences. Who cares about jail, prison, offenders?"

And she said to me, "You'd be surprised, Connie." My comfort zone was being challenged and I did not want to truly consider the possibilities of an unknown world.

In that very moment, I had diminished my MAGIC. I had minimized almost two decades of experience in the field of law-enforcement—specifically, Corrections—and I had dismissed all the hard work associated with my many academic achievements (and student loans).

It wasn't until days later that I thought more deeply about what I could possibly do to feel inspired again; to inspire others; to educate and to raise awareness. Finally, it hit me! At least I thought it did. I was going to write a book. Then I was paralyzed by this awful habit of second-guessing myself. The negative self-talk was relentless. I thought to myself: who is going to read this book, Connie? Again, who would be interested in you and your life journey? You're not famous, you're just a single mom who worked in the prison and did some "other" stuff. There I go again, getting in my own way. It seems that I do that often and I know I'm not alone in that.

Here I was in my nice little bubble. I knew I wanted more but I had no particular motivation to do the work to figure the "more" out. There was no imminent danger, so I was comfortable. I was ok dealing with the nagging feeling of wanting more; I excelled at ignoring it. Here's the thing about the comfort zone cage, you can waste a great deal of time there because it is what is familiar, and you know every nook and cranny of that cage.

As Steve Jobs once said, "Your time is limited so don't waste it living someone else's life. Don't be trapped by dogma— which is living with the results of other people's thinking. Don't let the noise of other's opinions drown out your inner voice. And most important, have the courage to follow your heart and intuition."

One morning, I got up and decided to get out of my own way and I began to talk to people about the possibility of doing a podcast. I knew that once I started speaking life into my ideas, the universe would assist me. I talked to a few friends about podcasts and received such great feedback about them. It seemed to me that a podcast would be good. It would allow me to share my learning without having to be in front of people.

I knew that once I started speaking life into my ideas, the universe would assist me.

All right, so the podcast sounded pretty simple but let me be real here, I had no idea what I was doing nor did I know anything about podcasting. I could have easily been discouraged and, though I knew nothing about nothing, I did what I knew how to do best: researched, researched, researched. There were many considerations, including subject matter experts, available content, content creation, the appropriate platform, and any technical expertise that would be required. These were waters I'd never navigated. Figuring out this new world was one thing, actually doing it was a whole other ball game.

My point here is that once you've acknowledged a cage, it is ok to take baby steps to get out of it. Those little steps will turn into big steps that get you closer to your freedom. This is a critical period in the process, so be patient with yourself as you accept your cage and decide that your time for change is now. ***Acknowledgement*** of the cage is the first phase in conquering it.

You cannot hesitate to familiarize yourself with your cage once you've truly acknowledged it as something that has been holding you back. Looking at it through that lens makes it look different. You will discover a million ways your cage has been preventing you from learning and growing. That is when you can plan on your transition out. Making that decision will require you to take action. What that looks like will be different for all of us.

This is a critical period in the process, so be patient with yourself as you accept your cage and decide that your time for change is now.

The ***heavy lifting*** is a serious time. It may require you to break some habits, to challenge belief systems, to dig deep and deal with some hurts that you've been holding on to. For me, a "friend" once said to me, "Connie, you have way more than many others. Will you never be satisfied with what you've already accomplished?" That always stayed with me. It was a thought that came to mind anytime I decided I was going to do something else. I had to acknowledge that the comment came from someone I cared about. I had to take the power from the statement and the person. Ultimately, I had to let go of the value that I gave that relationship, effectively neutralizing the comment.

Back to the podcast for a second. I thought I was done, I had decided. Now I was faced with a new learning opportunity. In this **heavy lifting** phase, you may be required to gain new skills in order to successfully move forward. Did I need to invest in all the fancy equipment? Did I need to book studio time? Would I need to hire a professional who could edit for me? In that very moment, I had to pause and say, "Lord, this is quite a daunting task. If this is where you want me to be and if this is what you want me to do, you need to show me the way. Place the people in my path who you know can and will help me."

Literally, the next day I found an app called Anchor. Anchor was everything. The app had the intros and outros, trimming ability, posting to multiple platforms upon completion, and an advertising component. So, I taught myself how to do it and *The Fly Behind the Wall* podcast was born, **VICTORY**! I had done it. It was fun, it was informative, it raised awareness, and folks started reaching out to me to ask questions about what they should do. I was taken aback by the fact that there was an actual interest.

Now, I didn't have thousands of listeners subscribing but I had introduced my voice and perspectives to the world. Somehow, I had just enough of the right people asking me questions. I think it would be important to add here that having completed the UCONN Executive MBA, my mind was opened to identifying gaps in a market and coming up with ways to fill that gap while earning a living. It also taught me about risks and liabilities, despite the best of intentions. Here I was giving out advice, for free, that if applied incorrectly could possibly open me up to some legal ramifications. At least, that's what I thought at that time.

One thing you will learn about me is that I am very effective at convincing myself that I can't do something. Have you mastered that as well? I will literally find every justification under the sun to build the case for why staying in my comfort zone would be the best thing for me. I know I am not alone in this. Is this a bad habit that we have in common? Hopefully, my story will inspire you to correct those bad habits and have more faith in yourself.

The beautiful thing about the comfort zone cage is that it keeps us blissfully ignorant. Though our minds may be trying to get us moving in another direction, there is no comfort like that comfy old couch. Stepping out of your comfort zone is hard. How many of us won't try something new because it makes us uncomfortable? It may challenge the belief system we have operated from our entire lives, and that's ok. There will come a point when the comfort zone is no longer comfortable, when that couch will start to feel bumpy and those once comforting words will sound unpleasant and distressing. Then you will know, it's time.

Are you ready to surrender what you are for what you could become?

Chapter 2

The Familial Cage

"In every conceivable manner, the family is the link to our past, bridge to our future."

— ALEX HALEY

My family's opinions of me matter. Their opinions of what I do matter. I am thankful to not have had the pressure of conforming to any expectations that they might have had of me, but I must acknowledge the influence they have in my life and the fact that I could have been caged by their expectations.

Coming from a very religious and spiritual background, there was a way my folks expected me to engage in the world. I always held onto my spiritual upbringing but knew there could be some limits placed on me if I never stepped out of the church to see what else the world had to offer.

Let me expand a bit on this Familial Cage.

Let's take smokers for example, a child is more likely to smoke if one parent is an active smoker—and that likelihood rises if both parents smoke. The younger and longer a child is exposed, the more likely they are to become smokers themselves. It's the passive influence that families can have on your life decisions that I want to highlight.

Consider a family of law enforcement professionals, where grandfather, father, mother, etc. are/were all in the industry. There just might be some explicit expectations of you in this scenario. It can be difficult going against the grain and stepping away from the expectations of the family. Many who find themselves in this situation, have other interests but feel they need to stay the course to honor their legacy.

Now, can they step out and try something new on their own? Of course, they can. But in comes that Cage of Comfort that reminds them that they know the industry, they've lived it all of their lives. They are also faced with the fear of disappointing themselves and their family; the fear of judgment; and the possibility of failing or falling, without the security blanket of their family name.

Once you acknowledge the legacy as a cage, you start to *discover* all the ways that it has stifled your growth. You want to also be real with yourself and acknowledge all of the privilege you might have benefitted from with that same family name.

Once you acknowledge the legacy as a cage, you start to discover all the ways that it has stifled your growth.

Can you succeed on your own?

Please do not misunderstand me here: I have a tremendous appreciation for a legacy. But for those who feel like they had no choice, it may feel very different.

Now, there is no way I could exclude spouses and children from the Familial Cage. Working behind the wall, sometimes means putting up walls to protect your family from the harsh realities that you work in—realities that you never talk about. Though you want to protect them, you have to acknowledge that you are excluding them from an important aspect of your life. Because you love and care about your family, you struggle to meet their expectations so they can experience an as-close-to normal version of you as possible.

It would be ill-advised for me to stop there. I'd like to mention how trapped some may feel when their relationship with their spouse is put to the test due to this profession. They struggle to meet the expectation of working "normal" hours or coming straight home. It is difficult to work "normal" hours when you have no control over your schedule or incidents that tend to happen right at the end of your scheduled shift, and then you get hit with mandatory overtime. This cage takes a hold and it's hard to break free without losing all that love along the way. To my point, it is an occupation with a 46.9% divorce rate.

When you have come to terms with the details of the cage, the *heavy lifting* begins. It's about taking action and dealing with all of your own feelings and emotions, which can be a struggle. You will need to have some crucial conversations with your family about your desire to stay or change course. Those will be emotionally strenuous conversations, but I recommend honesty and transparency so that there are no misunderstandings about your position and intentions. That weight that you have been carrying around on your shoulders will begin to get lighter. Though the decision to shift gears was frightening, we must celebrate the decision and the fact that you had the courage to have the conversation, *VICTORY!*

Me, Constantine Alleyne, was born to Maureen Linder and Cleveland C. Linder. I am a sister to five siblings and a mother to my beautiful daughter. My parents were/are hard

That weight that you have been carrying around on your shoulders will begin to get lighter.

workers. My dad is the son of sharecroppers, and my mom is an immigrant from Barbados. They wanted their children to graduate high school and make a good living. They themselves were not college grads and they did not push us to go to college.

Though education was important to my parents, we were allowed to choose. My oldest brother chose working, the second oldest chose a career in the military, I chose college and probably set the stage for my younger brother, who also chose college. My two sisters chose their own paths. I am a first-generation college graduate and the first of my parents' children to go to college. Therefore, I had absolutely no idea what I was doing.

I attended Midwood High School in Brooklyn, N.Y. My mom was happy when I graduated high school without being a teen pregnancy statistic—a sad reality of the 90s. I remember going to my guidance counselor and asking about college: what was it and how do I get in? My grades were always really good, not because I was preparing for college but because I had a mother who was really strict, and her expectation was that I always got straight A's. The counselor gave me all the guidance he could and sent me off to apply. I applied to Stony Brook University, which was close enough to home but far enough away from my family for me to have some freedom.

I do not believe my undergrad experience was any different from anyone else in that I was away from home for the first time and embraced my newfound freedom. I failed a class or two and was thrust back to reality. My status was matriculated but undecided for a while, but finally as I began to grow and mature, I found myself deciding on a bachelor's degree in African Studies; the best decision I ever made. Charles F. Glassman said it best, "Before I can become an expert on anything, I must first become an expert on me." I learned so much about myself, about my culture, about my history, about life.

During my senior year of college, my grandmother had triple bypass heart surgery that completely devastated me. Glendora Costello was my grandmother and she was a Guyanese governess who loved me to pieces. We talked all the time, she made me laugh, she made all my friends laugh, and she loved my mother just like she was her biological daughter. She was my grandmother in every sense of the word.

After her heart surgery it was hard for my grand-mother to get around and do the things she used to do; though, she tried to hold on to her independence for as long as possible. Once I graduated college, I moved back home, and I lived with her. My mom and I took care of her until her final transition. It was the journey of taking care of a homebound loved one that pushed me into Long Island University where I would obtain a Master's in Public Health. I wanted to be in a position where I could influence and implement policy change for vulnerable populations, including the geriatric.

I started working in a nursing home so I could see first-hand the impact of the various policies on the geriatric population. I found myself getting too close to the patients because I missed my grandmother and ultimately decided to leave because from week to week as patients died, I was experiencing the pain of losing my grandmother over and over again. I decided not to work for a few months but knew that when I did return to work, I wanted to be in a space where I could see the impact of policies on vulnerable pop-ulations.

Now, it is not my intention to simply talk about my family, but to highlight how family dynamics can influence your decisions either way. We can agree that we do not all have the same concept of family, but in general, there is respect for the structure of family. If you hold your family and their expectations of you in high regard, and you are not content with where you are, you have some work to do.

Family members have the best of intention when sharing their insights and opinions. What would have worked for them, during the time at which they were making their decisions, may not necessarily work for you or be the best option for you. You can appreciate their perspective, but you are under no obligation to do what they would do. It is when their missed opportunities become your load to carry that the Familial Cage takes up residence in your mind. That is not the lens through which you want to consider your future decisions. Be acutely aware of when the family expectations become your priority, as opposed to what would be in your best interest.

Phase II: Discovery

Chapter 3

My Cocoon: A Physical Cage

"A 'good job' can be both practically attractive while still not good enough to devote your entire life to."
— ALAIN DE BOTTON

It was the year 2000, I was looking for a job in the New York Times and I came across an ad posted by the New York City Health and Hospitals Corporation looking for Discharge Planners. I thought, great, you will be in a hospital setting and you will be preparing patients for their transitions back home. So, I sent in my resume, via fax, and was called in just a few days.

I was excited until the person on the other end said, "Are you familiar with Rikers Island?" I had no idea what Rikers Island was or where it was located.

I replied, "No, but I'm sure I can find it." The recruiter gave me an address, instructions as to how I was going to get to said island and where she would meet me upon arrival. Who knew??

For those of you who may not know what Rikers

Island is, it is the NYC jail system. There are several correctional centers on the island, housing offenders who are pre-trial or have been sentenced to one year or less for their offense. Though I was not an inmate, this jail/ work environment was my first cage, just as your job environment might be yours.

Does your work environment feel like a cage to you, like a place where your growth is being stunted and you can't spread your wings? If you are feeling like you can't seem to move up the corporate ladder or the chain of command, you are having a cage experience.

Many people get jobs that at some point in time were something they enjoyed doing or maybe it was always just a means to an end. When we lose interest in our work, we show up, but are not present. Our employers are paying for a warm body sitting at a workstation as opposed to an engaged employee thinking of how to innovate. When work starts feeling like a cage, we see high turnover, we see high absenteeism, we see low customer/consumer satisfaction ratings, and bottom lines that become stagnant.

TACTICAL PAUSE! I am going to ask you to bear with me as we move through this section of my journey. Given the complex nature of this cage, it is vital that I set the backdrop for what working in prison is like. Only then, will you fully understand and appreciate the transformative nature of this cage. Additionally, it is also important that I teach you a bit about the inner workings of the correctional system here in the United States.

So, get your pen, paper, and/or highlighters and I promise that the intricacies herein will give you insight into what was needed to conquer this cage.

For me, it took a long while for me to feel caged, because there was no day like the day before in jail. Until this point in my life, I was sheltered and had no idea what I was walking **Given the complex nature of this cage, it is vital that I set the backdrop for what working in prison is like. Only then, will you fully understand and appreciate the transformative nature of this cage.** into. I had no concept of the danger that lay behind the wall. Who knew how driving across that bridge would impact my life? I interviewed. I was hired. That was it. I was a Discharge Planner on Rikers Island and my role would be assisting mentally ill offenders' transitions back into the community. This is currently known as "re-entry."

I remember going to my parents' home and letting them know I was going to be starting this new job on Rikers Island—allowing for the entrance of the familial influence. I told them how I would be helping offenders transition back into the community; I created this wonderful narrative that I thought would help them accept me going into a jail every day.

My mother said, "None of my sons have ever darkened the doorway of a prison and my only biological daughter is now *volunteering* to go there. Where did I go wrong?"

In that very moment, I could have easily slipped into my Familial Cage because I did not want to disappoint or worry my mother. I had so much respect for her and her life experiences, the last thing I wanted to do was go against her. I remember explaining to her that she didn't go wrong anywhere, that I would be able to help individuals that look like my father, my brothers, my uncles, her sons. I would be able to take my life experiences and my education to a place where it is needed most.

I could tell that my mother did not like it, but she understood. Having grown up in the church, I decided to take it a step further and say, "Mommy, I would be one of the saints in Caesar's household."

We never talked about my decision again; instead, she prayed for me, day in and day out. There is nothing like a praying mother. I was able to drive back-and-forth across that bridge, walk through multiple facilities at all different security levels, and not be harmed. I do not take for granted a ten-year stint on Rikers Island with zero incidents.

Even with all my mother's prayers, there was absolutely nothing that could prepare me for my day one at Rikers Island. When I first drove past LaGuardia airport, made that right turn into the Rikers Island parking lot, and took my ID and registration to the first control center to get a pass to drive across the bridge, I figured that was it. Nope! I then had to drive across the bridge, find a parking space, walk to and through another control center, and wait for the route three and/or five bus that would drive me to OBCC

(Otis Bantum Correctional Center), where the manager was supposed to meet me at the front door and walk with me to Brad H. Discharge Planning office. It was an exhausting way to start my day. Was I really going to be able to do this every day?

No one was there to meet me when I finally arrived. Let me remind you that I have no experience with this population, I have minimal life experience, and no street savvy. This facility holds the Department of Correction's Central Punitive Segregation Unit, also known as the Bing, which can house 400 offenders. Please note, inmates and offenders are the same. There is an ongoing debate as to how we should refer to inmates as there are negative connotations associated with the word "inmate." For some, it's po-tae-to vs. po-ta-to. As to not offend anyone's sensitivities, I will go with "offender."

Offenders at this facility can be housed in dormitories or cells. I decided to go inside anyway and simply ask the very nice folks for some directions. The culture shock was more of a tsunami. I was greeted by an officer yelling at me to put my bag through the machine and step through the magnetometer, I was holding up the morning rush to get in as it was the start of shift. I went through the magnetometer and I was wanded. I walked into this small corridor where officers in central control sat. The gates closed behind me and when the gates in front of me opened everyone disbursed into their respective areas. I KNOW I looked lost. I asked an officer where the clinic was and he pointed me in that direction, not before giving me some unsolicited, sage advice. He said to me I couldn't walk around looking "brand new" because the offenders would eat me up and that I would be fresh meat to the officers.

Was it too late to turn back? That's all I could think. *How do I get out?* I was so turned around, I figured it best to go in the clinic, find the officer, and regroup.

I eventually walk up to the clinic officer and ask him for the Discharge Planning office. He stopped me abruptly and asked who I was. I was a face he did not know, and he knows all the faces that come into his clinic. Once I introduced myself, he softened a bit and escorted me to my office. He held the key to lock and unlock the office; civilians were not given any keys. It was a scary thought to know that once I stepped into the facility, I had to depend on someone else for my freedom. There were no windows, the walls were painted gray and had layers of dust on them that made them look even darker.

As I sat in the office for a few hours, I could feel the anxiety building. I contacted the Executive Director after the first hour because I figured they must have forgotten I was there. It turned out that the manager who was supposed to meet me was addressing an offender crisis that had taken place in another building. What they thought would take a few minutes turned into a full-on facility lockdown that prevented the manager from leaving the facility and coming over to meet me.

In an effort to calm my nerves, I decided I would clean. I went to the clinic officer and asked for cleaning supplies so I could clean my office. He gave me the supplies, but not without first giving me a lecture on how my department needed to order its own supplies as we had separate budgets… Though I worked within the confines of the Department of Corrections, my salary came from the New York City Department of Health and Mental Hygiene who held the contract to provide Discharge Planning services—a distinction that was clearly important for me to know.

My supervisor finally arrived and acted as though I hadn't been sitting in this strange place for hours without direction. He just jumped in with no apologies. He let me know that I would learn that from day-to-day all kinds of things would happen that he could never prepare me for. And, more often than not, nothing would go as planned. He went on to say that I would need to plan for any type of operational disruptions that would make me late because that was all I would have control of.

From that day on, I accepted the reality my supervisor warned me of as a part of my work life. We went on to have an in-depth conversation about offenders, the culture of Rikers Island, and the culture of offenders and their manipulative behaviors. There was very little instruction on how to do my job. We talked a lot about safety and security. He wanted to make sure that I understood we were in their house, referring to custody, and what they say goes.

It was a very eye-opening first day, to say the least.

On day two, I at least knew what to expect from the

perspective of getting a pass to drive over the bridge, taking the route bus to the facility, and knowing where to go once I got off the bus.

On my second day, my manager was there, thank God! We talked about my day one experience and then we began to discuss work itself. I had no idea that any such program had ever existed. Here was this court-mandated program put in place because a mentally ill ex-offender hit someone over the head with a brick in Manhattan. Apparently, he'd sought out treatment but never got it because either he didn't have the mental capacity to advocate for himself or he didn't have the necessary medical insurance to cover his mental health needs. The city's response to the incident was this Brad H. Discharge Planning Program.

Just to give some context here of what I'd gotten myself into: New York City is home to one of the largest jail systems in the United States—second only to the Los Angeles jail system. The New York City Department of Correction provides for the care of individuals accused of crimes, as well as those convicted and sentenced to one year or less of jail time. Besides the holding facilities located in the criminal, supreme, and family court houses across the city, there are fifteen different offender facilities throughout New York: ten are located on Rikers Island. The remaining five include the borough facilities in Manhattan, the Bronx (a five-story barge) and Brooklyn, as well as hospital wards at the Health and Hospitals Corporation's (HHC) Elmhurst and Bellevue facilities.

The jail population was on a steady decline three

years after I started, so beginning in 2003. However, the number of offenders with a mental health diagnosis had increased during the same period. In 2009, the daily population of city jails averaged 13,362 and of these 27 percent (3,607 offenders) had some kind of mental health diagnosis; in 2012, the average daily population of the jails had declined to 12,287, while the share of this population with a mental health diagnosis had increased to slightly more than a third (4,177 offenders).

A large and growing number of offenders with mental health diagnoses in correctional facilities is not unique to New York City, but rather is a problem throughout much of the country. Comprehensive national data on this problem are scarce; nor is there even a standardized definition or measure of mental illness in the correctional context. One often-cited 2006 study by the Federal Bureau of Justice Statistics, found that more than half of all prison and jail offenders incarcerated in the United States had some type of mental health problem, with the largest percentage found in local jails. Three jails—Chicago's Cook County Jail, the Los Angeles County Jail, and New York City's Rikers Island—now comprise the three largest mental health institutions in the country.

Brad H. Litigation and Settlement was the driver for this new position. City and state officials have been grappling with the problem of mentally ill individuals in the criminal justice system for at least the past fifteen years. In 1999, the Urban Justice Center, Debevoise & Plimpton LLP, and New York Lawyers for the Public Interest filed a class-action lawsuit on behalf of seven plaintiffs who had all been arrested multiple times and received mental health treatment while incarcerated but were never given a discharge plan upon release.

The lawsuit challenged New York City's practice of discharging people with psychiatric disabilities from the city jails in the middle of the night with only $1.50 and two subway tokens, and without any medication or referral to services. Failure to provide discharge planning in the jails was determined to be a violation of New York State Mental Hygiene Law 29.15, which mandates "providers of inpatient health services to provide discharge planning."

A settlement with the plaintiffs was reached that took effect in 2003. The city agreed to provide comprehensive discharge planning to all offenders who qualify as a member of the protected class. A class member is defined as an offender whose period of confinement in city jails lasts twenty-four hours or longer, and who during confinement receives treatment for a mental illness.

Rikers Island was no walk in the park. I went from day-to-day learning to even more learning. I had the benefit of great tutelage from officers who saw I was struggling to reconcile what I was seeing with what I had known to be a reality of life. I think they could also see I had ZERO street sense; I was "ripe for the picking." Though, I had no idea what that even meant until I started working there.

I quickly learned that "ripe for the picking" means I was the perfect target for offender manipulations. I sincerely wanted to help everyone, and I was gullible to all the stories I was told in the beginning, but then I caught on to everything—all the games, all the lies, and all the stories. This is not to say there were not some genuine, heart wrenching stories, but those were few and far between.

For the most part, the offenders were usually angling for something, secondary gain was the name of the game. The angle could be a pen, a cigarette, a candy, some kind of ointment, a phone call on an unmonitored office phone, or simply the ability to use the restroom in private. Go figure!

You might be thinking why the restroom is important... See, in prison/jail, the offenders don't get to use the restroom in private. Depending on whether they live in a dorm or they live in cells, their toilet may literally be five steps from their bunk bed. So, they use the bathroom with their cellmate nearby.

Another point of clarity: We may use the terms jail and prison interchangeably, but there is a difference. A jail is usually in the city and essentially houses individuals who are sentenced less than one year or who are detainees that are going back-and-forth to court in an attempt to fight the trial, so you would call those pre-trial detainees. In jails, 74 percent of people held are not convicted of any crime. If you include the 115,000 people held in local jails that rent out space to other agencies, 65 percent of people in jail are convicted. Either way jail incarceration rates are driven largely by local bail practices. Prisons usually house people who are sentenced for more than a year and they must serve a longer sentence.

Last I read, there were 2.5 million people incarcerated in prisons and jails. According to 2020 research of Prisonpolicy.org, the American criminal justice system holds almost 2.3 million people in 1833 state prisons, 110 federal prisons, 1772 juvenile correctional facilities, 3134 local jails, 218 immigration detention facilities, and 80 Indian country jails, as well as in military presence civil commitment centers, state psychiatric hospitals, and prisons in the U.S. territories. Jail represents nearly all Americans' initial contact with corrections.

The public health practitioner in me truly enjoys sifting through the research and has a great appreciation for those who are studying the various prison initiatives, as well as the impact that those initiatives are having on the population and community.

The biggest challenge we face is not with the data collection and presentation of the findings, but the context that the audience has when they are reading. Most people do not have an accurate lens through which to view prison issues; in my opinion, context is vital. Movies and TV series like *Oz, Orange is the New Black, The Wire, Green Mile,* and *Shawshank Redemption* are typically the most popular lens through which people relate to the prison experience. While the stories told have merit, the depictions pale in comparison to the everyday experience. The advantage I have when reading these comprehensive reports is my first-hand engagement with the populations and the environment.

Every aspect of this chapter was about discovering, learning, and understanding the intricacies of my physical cage, which happened to be a jail. The key to *discovery* is being able to synthesize the information. What did it all mean? Did I know enough about the bigger picture to draw any meaningful conclusions or make any informed decisions? In a system of this complex nature, I would say no. I did not know enough; it was all still new and very exciting.

I will later speak of another physical cage experienced by victims of domestic violence. The home provided by their abuser served as a physical cage that they were not allowed to leave from day to day. But your physical cage may not be as dramatic as a prison or the home of an abuser, it could just be your body.

Think about it, how many times have you put something off because you want to lose ten or twenty pounds before you feel confident enough? We allow our bodies to dictate the way we engage with the world. Consider your desk. Many of us struggle to move from behind our desks and leave our offices. Micromanaging bosses may drive this behavior.

You always have a choice to engage in that *heavy lifting*.

Chapter 4

The Cage of Innocence

"Keep your innocence and ignorance aside, and expose yourself to dangerous situations, and understand the deeper secrets of life."
— MICHAEL BASSEY JOHNSON

I was twenty-five years old when the physical cage had become my cocoon. Who knew what was developing inside, or *who* was developing inside? The mental transformation was underway. Sometimes we get ourselves into situations unknowing of the possible outcomes. Sometimes we know the outcomes and go in thinking that we will be the exception to the rule. In my case, I just wanted to help people. I did not know the various manipulative tactics I would encounter, the violence, uncertainty, ambiguity, or complexity of the system.

Naivety, the gift and the curse. Remember when you first started your job? I'm sure that the learning journey wasn't easy, but you were allowed to learn from your mistakes. Those are the lessons you will never forget. You should be curious about how things work and how your role fits into the bigger picture. Some of us need that in order to understand how important their role is in the grand scheme of things. For others, it doesn't really matter because they are struggling to grasp the simpler details of the job.

I was going to be planning offender discharges. I had no clue what that meant but I was on the frontline of what we now know to be mass incarceration. Discharge planning involved contacting the community resources to ensure that offenders could continue medical, mental health, and substance abuse treatment in the community; completing a medical assistance program application; securing housing; and contacting families to smooth over burned bridges. Today, discharge planning is called re-entry and those efforts trying to reconstruct those burnt bridges is now known as family reunification efforts. Aligning offenders with viable benefit options in the marketplace is what is done in many systems. Though times have changed, so much is still the same.

Motivational interviewing was the approach that we took to garner engagement. There was no way for us to fully implement the discharge plan beyond the wall. This method increased the effectiveness of our correctional treatment plan by having us interact with the offender in ways that promoted them having a stake in the change process, despite their level of prisonization. For those that do not know, prisonization is the process by which an incarcerated person absorbs the customs of prison society and learns to adapt to the environment.

This discharge planning effort did not happen without the support of other correctional professionals, including mental health who managed the treatment process. They prescribed psychotropic medications, as clinically indicated, and employed a range of treatment modalities. Reality therapy was a common one, it is the treatment that emphasizes personal responsibility for actions and their consequences. Many of the guys were disconnected from the reality of the impact of their behaviors on their family and friends.

Most of the individuals I encountered were looking for a way out. They saw in me a future that they could have and wanted me to help them get there. There were limits to how much support I could provide and how much advocating I could do. The good days were those days when I could see that I had inspired someone. I could see the hope awakened in their eyes; the wheels of change turning in their minds. The bad days were those where you could see the despair in their cheeks; there was no color in sight and no emotion in their voices. Those days motivated me to dig deeper into my limited tool chest. As I explored my mental landscape, I carved out a path for those who thought there was no path for them.

They saw in me a future that they could have and wanted me to help them get there.

"The transformation from mediocrity to excellence requires a soul searching and life altering incubation," said Piyush Kamal. Not only was I in a life altering incubation, but so were the offenders. I was there to guide them through all of their soul searching. These guys were trying to figure out how to talk to their children, what they could do to get their GED and possibly go to a community college. Many of them did not feel worthy of any opportunity for redemption.

I am here to tell you that some of their past transgressions were gruesome, but they were not giving up on themselves. Behind the wall, many of them were having their very own metamorphosis. These offenders were doing the *heavy lifting*, tackling past hurts from a phone attached to a cement block. It was confirmation for me that when you have made the decision to change your life, there is nothing that can stop you. If, in one of the harshest of environments, an offender can find hope, so can you!

My reality behind the wall was not all cupcakes and rainbows. I was a young woman who had to ward off all sorts of inappropriate advances. That was ALL on-the-job

It was confirmation for me that when you have made the decision to change your life, there is nothing that can stop you.

training. The battle between setting boundaries and my timidity was an everyday challenge. I had to find my voice, learn how to assert myself and redirect the offenders and their inappropriate comments. When we talk about inmate manipulation, we must understand that it is a slow and subtle process. It is knowing that today's request will escalate to something grander the next time if you comply.

I had my secretary fall victim to the manipulation. The crazy thing about it is that she was not a service provider. She had absolutely no reason to ever engage in conversation with an offender. I recall seeing her have an exchange with an offender and I asked her what he wanted. She went into this elaborate explanation of her trying to explain the services we offered to him. At the time, she had given me no reason not to trust her.

I had left the office for the day when I got a call on my cell from the Clinic Captain. He said, "Connie, I hope you didn't make it too far." Thankfully, I had not. I had to turn around and head back to the facility. Can you guess what happened? My secretary was being walked out for putting cigarettes (contraband) in a discharge planning brochure and placing the brochure in the garbage for the offender. This was a grown woman!

What was she thinking?

It turns out that on multiple days, after I would leave the office, she was seen having quick exchanges with this offender. It started with a tissue, another day a cough drop, then a pencil and now, cigarettes. Apparently, the offender had expressed an interest in discharge planning services but did not qualify. He gave her this sob story which pulled on her heartstrings. She told him she would see if one of the discharge planners would see him. She was hooked, in her mind she was going to be his savior, and in his mind, she was going to be his mule.

Custody did their due diligence and on one faithful day they decided to let him go to the clinic, do whatever he was going to do, and pull him into the bullpen to search him before allowing him to return to his housing unit. Low and behold he had the discharge planning brochure and cigarettes on his person. It did not take much for him to start singing. All they did was tell him that he would be receiving additional charges and the time would be consecutive not concurrent.

My secretary was walked out and had to deal with the legal consequences. I do not know what became of it as she was stripped of everything and escorted off the island. She had to learn that the offenders have loyalty to only themselves.

The look on her face as she was being escorted out was pitiful. She had a husband and children, for crying out loud. How do you explain that kind of mess to your family? There was nothing I could do for her. I called my Executive Director and let him know what had happened. I'll never forget, he said, "Well, she dug her own grave."

I learned the ugly side of things but chose to focus on the side of things I had control over. After a while, this role became more to me than just a job. I recall one of my African Studies courses with Professor Macado at SUNY Stony Brook, where we had to read a book called *The Black Family* by Roberts Staples. There is a chapter that stands out called "The Black Male: Searching Beyond Stereotypes," by Manning Marable. This excerpt seemed to come alive for me, it reads:

> What is a black man in an institutional racist society, in the social system of mod-ern America, the essential tragedy of being

black and male is our inability, as men and as people of African descent, to define ourselves without the stereotypes which the larger society imposes upon us, and through various institutional means perpetuates and permeates within our entire culture. Our relations with our sisters, our parents, and children and indeed across the entire spectrum of human relations, are imprisoned by images of the past, false distortions which seldom if ever capture the essence of our being. We cannot come to terms with black women until we understand the half-hidden stereotypes which have crippled our development and social consciousness. We cannot challenge racial and sexual inequality, both within the black community and across the larger American society, unless we comprehend the critical difference between the myths about ourselves and the harsh reality of being a black man.

I could not ignore what I had learned on the other side of the wall; this was more personal than I anticipated it would be. I have three black brothers and a black father, who at any given moment could have been one bad decision away from incarceration. The task of assisting these men to get back on their feet was one I did not take lightly. It became more of a responsibility than just a job; it became more personal—which, by the way, is an occupational hazard when working in prison.

In this place and in this space, I was becoming. My

depth of focus changed. I realized what I was doing was going to impact the black family, not just the one individual who would be sitting at my desk. I was going to impact generations to come. I could be the reason why intergenerational incarceration is halted within the families I reached. As I learned more about the plight of the offender, I realized that my work was not in vain. With this realization came an awareness of the gravity of my role; dare I say the **discovery** of my purpose?

Suicide. Yes, you heard me, *suicide.* Never could I imagine that this would be an experience of mine behind the wall. I was in my office, minding my business when I looked out my door and saw an offender hanging from the ceiling of the bathroom. I could not believe what I was witnessing. I ran to the door and called out to the clinic officer that someone was hanging. He ran down the hall to attend to the offender while calling for backup.

As I stood there in shock, I felt a chill move down my body. I had never had a literal hair-raising experience before. Someone had just tried to take their life outside my office. His eyes were bulging, and I could see the veins begin to bulge in his head and neck. He urinated on himself as one officer lifted to relieve the pressure around his neck so the other officer could cut the t-shirt that he had fashioned into a noose. I could not believe this was happening.

What could have been going through his mind or in his life to bring him to the point of taking his life? Was he mentally unstable? Was he under the influence of a black-market concoction? Did I mention that I was standing there in disbelief? Ok, so I just want to be clear that this is **not** a normal experience. Though I became a NYS Emergency Medical Technician early on in my career, this was not something I could mentally prepare for nor did I want to be prepared for it. Quite frankly, I would be good if it never happened again. Be that as it may, this young man needed help.

There was absolutely no way I could make it through the rest of my workday. The image of the inmate hanging had stained my conscience. There was no critical incident debriefing, just a request for me to write a report about what I had seen. No one asked if I was ok or if I needed to speak to a mental health professional. All I could think was that this was business as usual for those who have experience with this sort of thing and for me it was devastation. I did not know that offender. What I knew was that he had decided he would have been better off dead than alive. It's saddening to know that he was not the only one. Life behind the wall can trigger suicidal ideations in both offenders and correctional staff. The suicide rate of correctional professionals is quite unnerving.

Back to purpose, was I supposed to be there to interrupt this attempt he made on his life? Witnessing a suicide attempt was something that hurt me to my core. You know? That cry a kid has when they are so hurt no sound comes out, but tears are rolling, and their mouth is open? That is what I felt like inside.

I mentioned this being personal. Now let me be clear about what I mean by *personal*. I was not taking work home with me, nor was I overextending myself into undue familiarity territory. I was doing my best to make sure that these men had a fighting chance for a successful transition. For those who really wanted to reunite with their families, I was providing the necessary counsel needed for them to make things right. Another thing that I think is important to note here is that as a service provider it is critical that you ensure there are no orders of protection against the offender and that you are not in any way violating said order by trying to reunite that offender with someone they shouldn't be in contact with. In all cases due diligence is essential.

Regardless of how passionate I was, I could never forget the prison culture I was working in and the offender subculture. During the past fifty years, as the population of the United States has changed, so has the prison population. The number of African Americans and Hispanics in prison has greatly increased. More people in prison come from urban areas, and more have been convicted of drug related and violent offenses. Incarcerated members of street gangs, which are often organized along racial lines, frequently regroup inside prison, and contribute to elevated levels of violence. Another major change has been a number of correctional officers who are members of public employee unions, along with their use of collective bargaining to improve working conditions, safety procedures, and training.

As the number of people in America's prisons increased substantially over the past three decades, tensions built within the overcrowded institutions.

Although today's correctional administration seeks to provide humane incarceration, they struggle with limited resources. The modern prison faces many of the difficult problems that come from other parts of the criminal justice system: racial conflict, legal issues, limited resources, and growing populations. Jails are the entryway to Corrections and despite the challenges, my role didn't change. All offenders had access to discharge planning services.

In addition to contending with the prison politics (bureaucracy) and offender subculture I had to learn to identify and navigate mental illness, substance abuse dependencies, and medical illnesses. Almost 2/3 of those in jail have a history of mental problems; for 1/5 of people in jails, there is a recent history of serious mental disorder. But many jails do not offer any form of psychological care at all, and only a minority receive any form of mental health treatment. Various disciplines put in their call down lists to see offenders throughout their day.

While facilities are short on resources, human resources that is, the reality is that those who are hired to provide services do their best to see those offenders that are within their scope of treatment. Caseloads simply were not manageable, and people fell through the cracks. Regardless of the never-ending case assignments, providers did and continue to do their best to make sure that the population is stable.

The Cage of Innocence was preparing me for the outside world. For ten years I was an attentive student of the profession. My *discovery* phase was full. The lessons I had learned behind the wall would prove to be invaluable. During this phase, it is all about learning. I had to be coachable! You never know what this phase will teach you. I had passively absorbed the culture and the games people play, offenders and staff. My time there taught me everything from mental health and substance abuse to the impact of socioeconomic status and racism. Learning how to adapt and adjust along the way was inevitable.

As you navigate your Cage of Innocence experience, be sure to take notes. You will need to refer to them as you advance to your next level. The lessons we learn first-hand will never be forgotten. Remember that in this Cage of Innocence you are allowed to be a novice, you're learning.

What are some of the key points you gleaned in your Cage of Innocence?

Phase III: Heavy Lifting

Chapter 5

Caged With Your Decisions

"The only walls that exist are those you have placed in your mind. And whatever obstacles you conceive, exist only because you have forgotten what you have already achieved."

— SUZY KASSEM

You know it is time to leave, time to move on, time to advance but you are just not ready. You can be given all the tools you need for success but when you are hesitant to use them, they are just tools. All too often we have what we need, we overthink what we need to do next and work ourselves up into a frenzy. It is ok to take that tactical pause. As a matter of fact, I was trained on a skill called tactical psychological first aid.

Psychological First Aid (PFA) is an evidence-informed modular approach to help children, adolescents, adults, and families in the immediate aftermath of disaster and terrorism. Individuals affected by a disaster or traumatic incident, whether survivors, witnesses, or responders to such events, may struggle with or face new challenges following the event. Sounds a bit harsh, I know. We must acknowledge the psychological impact that our cage experiences have on us; it's not pretty, though we come through them feeling renewed. For example, there is a very distinct smell behind the wall and when I happen to smell someone that smells like it, I am jolted back to my past prison life as if I were walking down one of the corridors.

Understand that this *heavy lifting* phase is no joke. Sometimes we minimize the cage experience so that we do not have to do the *heavy lifting* required to cope and heal. It is not my intention to add too much weight to this book but to ensure that we do not gloss over this crucial point in our journeys.

Sometimes we minimize the cage experience so that we do not have to do the *heavy lifting* required to cope and heal.

When offenders know they are going to be going home, it can be a very confusing time; they hesitate, too. The prison has been their cage for some time in their lives. For some, it is what they are most familiar with. They are super excited about the possibility of getting back to "the world" but scared because for them life has frozen in time, but it has not frozen in time for their family and friends. The world has moved on when they have not. It is a very sobering experience to be holding on to memories of your child when he/she was seven years old and then when you're released, they are now ten or twelve. The offender has missed years of growth and development that they cannot get back. Some have also been out of contact with their children during that incarceration period. Children and families have adjusted to life without the offender. That can be a very difficult reality for the offender. Everything they were once familiar with is now unfamiliar.

The *heavy lifting* required for them to rejoin their lives can depend on their mental and emotional states prior and post incarceration. Because they can be unrealistic in their expectations of their family and friends, their adjustment period can take months. They work to make amends with those they have hurt. We have to acknowledge the barriers presented by the stigma associated with being an ex-offender. Dealing with the judgment and society looking down on you is mentally and emotionally taxing. Those are just a few examples of the *heavy lifting* that they must do. Dare I mention the lifelong battle with addiction and mental illness. They have to build skills that can get them to a space where they are employable. For many of the offenders, it is just too hard for them to do it all on their own so they would rather be in jail/prison than be out in the real world where they are reminded daily that they are inadequate or ill-equipped to manage their own lives.

Now look at that cage! Many of them would rather be incarcerated because someone else is making all the decisions for their lives. Behind the wall, their inadequacies are normalized, and they are provided with the resources they need to function optimally, but without their freedom. Would you be willing to give up your freedom for shelter, three meals, free healthcare, and free cable television? As much as we talk about prison reform, we have to examine the power of the cage.

I recall meeting with one of the offenders and putting his discharge plan together. He was so excited about going home but he was nervous because he was aware that some things had changed while he was incarcerated. His biggest point of anxiety was the fact that he did not know what to do with the MetroCard. Before he went in, they were using tokens and the fact that there was this new technology that he was unfamiliar with made him extremely anxious. I could not minimize his fear of the unknown and risk him reoffending just to avoid it. Ultimately, I pulled up a copy of the MetroCard on my computer so that he could see what the MetroCard looked like and we talked about how the MetroCard was used.

Here I was planning for him to get connected to community resources and possibly going to college or community college since he already had a high school diploma and he couldn't get past what was going to happen when he got dropped off on the other side of the bridge in East Elmhurst.

Regardless of how great a plan is, if you are not ready, you're just not ready. Again, I will say, be patient with yourself and allow your growth and development to happen so that you can be ready. More *heavy lifting* to do. The sooner we recognize that there is no easy way out of the cage, the better off we will be.

"It is moments like these that force us to try harder, and dig deeper, and to discover gifts we never knew we had- to find the greatness that lies within each of us."
— BARACK OBAMA

You will have to make some extremely tough decisions. Those old beliefs won't get you to your new destination. Cutting loose some old relationships that have been holding you back may be the only solution. What kind of **heavy lifting** will you need to do? What doors do you need to close before you open the new one? Only you know what you are holding on to that is holding you back. No one can do the work for you.

Freedom. We enjoy the freedom we have. When you live within the confines of Corrections, you have little to no decisions to make. You are told when to wake up, when to shower, when to eat, when to watch tv, when to go to school or work and when you can go out for recreation. The majority of their daily activities are on a schedule—commissary, law library, service provider appointments, etc. You can decide to make a call, to write a letter, to accept a visit and to use the bathroom.

All of this can make the free world seem daunting and everyday life decisions overwhelming. These individuals had every decision made for them, requiring no critical thinking skill development for significant periods of time in their lives.

This is where re-entry initiatives come into play. The courts are designed to help returning citizens successfully "reenter" society following their incarceration;

thereby reducing recidivism, improving public safety, and saving money. There are some essentials that offenders need to be successful when they transition back into the community. We know they need access to transportation, clean clothing, documentation, financial resources, housing security, employment, education, and healthcare. They also need a support system: community-based programs, family members, and faith-based organizations.

Transportation, this is merely transportation to and from essential appointments, i.e. interviews, employment, parole/probation visits, treatment facilities, etc. It can also be particularly difficult to go out confidently to advocate for one's self in dirty clothes. Clean clothes are critical as far as their ability to engage in activities with the public in an appropriate manner and not be shunned.

Documentation is a necessity; they need to have access to a birth certificate, driver's license, or non-drivers identification; official, universally accepted forms of identification. Financial resources are essential for purchasing food, paying rent and utilities, and covering other daily living activities. My years of experience working with the population has taught me that self-sufficiency is the key. The tools we provide offenders upon release that help them be self-sufficient ARE the essentials. Not everyone wants to manipulate the system and not be a productive member of society. Not everyone is a crook, as they are commonly referred to behind the wall.

Participation in vocational and educational programs

in prison has been declining over the past decade, and only a minority of people in prison who need drug treatment receive it while incarcerated. Many who face release cannot identify the specific things they must avoid doing in order to stay out of trouble. There are very few employment programs that show promise for reducing recidivism. Employment-focused re-entry programs have had little success in reducing recidivism. This means that prisoner re-entry efforts that rely mainly on job training and subsidized jobs are not likely to succeed. Unfortunately, most offenders are unable to make a successful transition and eventually return to prison; proof that you cannot bypass the heavy lifting. It is part of the process to get you to VICTORY!

It was utterly frustrating to work for months with offenders on a plan in preparation for release and to turn around and see them back in custody within a matter of weeks; for some, it just took a weekend. When this happens, we must remind ourselves that relapse is a part of the recovery process. Many offenders choose to go back to familiar persons, places, and things; that NEVER works out well for them.

On the flip side, it was extremely rewarding when they never came back. I would love to believe that it was my plan and my commitment to their process. Somehow, I know that it was their personal decisions to make the change and break the cycle. Either way it is a **VICTORY**, for me professionally and for them personally.

I would continue this pattern of learning and devel-

oping myself so that I could better serve the population. Amid that, my colleagues thought that I could
be of value to them. They decided they would vote
me in to be a union delegate. Me? Clearly, they saw
something in me that I did not see in myself. How
could I possibly serve as a delegate? I was not particularly familiar with the union contract but learned the
contractual mandates.

I answered the call and became the delegate. Here's
the thing, I could not lose sight of what was right and
wrong. I encountered co-workers who were wrong
but wanted me to go fight their battles with management. That did not sit well with me, so I would express
my position to the employee and recommend that
they seek out an alternate delegate to represent their
interests. It was not a comfortable position to be in,
in my professional world. It was one of the first times
in my career where I had to set those professional
boundaries and sometimes stand alone on unpopular
issues. I believe that because I had a good relationship
with my co-workers, they knew I was always trying
to do what was right and not necessarily what was
popular.

In less than a year, my Executive Director called me
over to his facility and had a talk with me. I will never
forget this. He said, "Connie, you are a leader. I do not
want you to be buried in inmate matters too much
longer. I would like you to become a supervisor and
will recommend you for promotion."

While I was flattered, it took some time for me to
register that this man, who I admired from a distance,

recognized I had more to offer. He was willing to invest the time in developing me. I guess I could say he was one of my first mentors.

Certainly, I doubted I was ready for leadership, but I recognized this was a great opportunity for me. Who knew what this opportunity would lead to? Within nine months of employment, I was promoted to Health Services Manager and was supervising people who were once my co-workers.

As one could imagine, transitioning from colleague to manager came with its challenges. One thing that helped was the insistence that we were always professional and respectful in our exchanges and disagreements. I was naturally good at compartmentalizing and separating work matters from social matters. Simply put, at work we handled business, and outside of work we were friends. To this day, twenty years later, I am still close friends with that team.

After ten years of managing on Rikers Island, I decided that it was time to learn about the population from another angle. I also figured it was time that I diversified my resume a bit. Here's the thing, I was struggling to let go of this harsh environment that I had become so familiar with.

Even though I had found a new role, I told myself I needed a transition plan. I ended up working both full-time jobs, in leadership capacities. I worked at Rikers Island by day and my new job by night. I had the flexibility to swap days and nights to have a presence equally on both shifts.

As the beautiful icon Lena Horne once put it, *"It's not the load that breaks you down, it's the way you carry it."*

To say it was a stressful time would be a gross understatement of that experience. Admittedly, I was young, so I was happy with earning two, relatively sizable, full-time salaries but I knew I could not sustain this madness so I decided I would leave Rikers.

Now, writing this passage has forced me to acknowledge the weight I was carrying. My **heavy lifting** included the responsibility of overseeing the transition plans of thousands of offenders, managing over one hundred employees between the two organizations, managing the operational responsibilities of both organizations, and a new marriage. I needed to make some decisions and make them quick. I was not going to be able to carry that weight for too long.

The joke was on me. I was hired as the Residential Director for the Institute for Community Living. I know there is nothing funny about that, but as my fortune would have it, I was going to be covering the site that sits on the grounds of Creedmoor Psychiatric Center in Queens Village, NY. This center was where we sent many of our mentally ill offenders from Rikers Island and it turned out that many of my residents were former clients.

The good news was that I would be able to see these individuals post release and could assist in the implementation and execution of those discharge plans. I had a clinical team I could educate and train to continue the good work that the discharge planners were doing, given that there was no aftercare component to jail discharge planning.

You want to talk about divine intervention!

Anytime I question my purpose and the assignment on my life, I think of my journey and how God allowed me to come up with a plan but was certain to remind me that His hand was in the midst. I had the opportunity to see what happened behind the wall but here He was giving me a front row seat to what happens once they are discharged, giving me the power to influence their success upon release. If that wasn't confirmation that I was in the right place doing the right thing, I don't know what would have been.

This autonomy did not come without a price. I felt personally responsible for the success of my residents. I would meet with them to understand their needs and make sure our team was actually hearing them out and allowing them to play an active role in the development of their treatment plans. From what I was told, it was not customary for a Director to be involved with patient care. Directors would audit records from time-to-time and give feedback periodically but that was about it. In my time there, we moved away from the template approach to care because one size did not fit all. Caring about the success of our residents went beyond words, it was evident in our actions and the way we engaged the residents in conversation.

In the spirit of complete transparency, I neglected to mention that my *heavy lifting* included me being pregnant at this time, which is an important detail in this part of my story. The work I was doing bought me pure joy along with the life that was developing within. See, I had suffered multiple miscarriages while working on Rikers. I don't believe I **ever** acknowledged the impact that the cage had on my physical body. Could there have been something in the air of the island? Something behind those walls that my body was responding to? Just God saying not here, not now?

Transitioning off the island could have been my way of giving the possibility of new life a chance. My pregnancy also caused me to ponder the meaning of life and examine how my residents actually got to this place. I'm sure they were not all born to crack addicted parents who didn't give a crap about them. I wanted to create a world where people did not feel invisible or forgotten. I must say that this residential facility gave me that opportunity.

I got to know all my residents by name. I learned their psychosocial histories and understood their triggers. I implemented interdisciplinary treatment meetings so that we all knew the residents and were all in a position to be of assistance if the assigned Case Manager was absent when support was needed. The clinical team supported this approach of creating a net of support so that no one would fall through the cracks. This is not to say everything was cupcakes and rainbows every day, but the facility was stable, the staff was happy, and most importantly they felt supported.

I had an open-door policy for staff and residents, and I was visible. Pregnant and all, I would walk the floors of the facility and roll up my sleeves to help wherever needed. I do not subscribe to the train of thought that the supervisor should be untouchable or that the supervisor is above the work. I believe that is where many managers go wrong, it's also one of the differences between a manager and a leader. Suffice it to say, I enjoyed being able to serve in the manner that I served at the Institute for Community Living.

One night an unstable resident violently attacked one of my team while she was distributing medication. What a nightmare! It was one of those calls you hope you never have to get. Now seven months pregnant, I am rushing out of my home to drive to Queens to get knee deep in the crisis. I arrived at the crime scene. My staff person was rushed to the hospital, the resident was arrested, and now I have to gather as many details as possible to gain a full understanding of the event so that I can provide said details to my central office.

While handling the business of things, it was important to me that I attended to the people. Emotions were high, the staff and residents were worried about their safety and the well-being of the employee who was injured during the attack. It was equally important to me that the facility was secure, which was never a concern before this incident. Before I left to return home, I had reported to our central office, arranged to have a security expert come in and do a walk through, set up for EAP to come in and provide support to the team, and met with the residents to reassure them that we were going to do everything we could to keep them safe. I had never been in any such crisis before but one of the clinical leads followed me back to my office to ask how I was doing and commended me on the manner in which I handled things.

This was not a time that I could even think of myself. Safety was my focus. It was at this point that I realized my time and experiences behind the wall had prepared me to make decisions rapidly and effectively. Behind the wall, incidents would just pop off without warning. I developed a social intelligence that transcends my ability to put into words. I had a broad chamber of thought and had passively absorbed many skills and abilities from the environment. The implicit knowledge gained is not knowledge that could be taught to me or that I could teach to someone else, but it is there, and I tap into it involuntarily. I had developed practical intelligence and new ways of solving problems that I did not know were there.

In the days to come, I would manage the calls from the media and my manager. Rather, I would redirect the media to our central office who had a team dedicated to public communications. My primary concern was for my team. A member of our team was seriously injured. For me, it wasn't just some passing incident that needed to be managed for the sake of the business. It was difficult to shift back to business as usual. So, we didn't. We needed to deal with our trauma experience in a healthy way before we could go back to supporting our residents. I arranged for mental health professionals to come in and provide individual support to the team so that the healing could begin.

Before long we were on the path to a relatively healthy existence. That would not come without a great deal of *heavy lifting*. We all had to deal with our anger that one of us was attacked and our fear that it could have been any of us. We had to deal with the reality of the instability of our residents and for those who had experienced trauma in their pasts, this brought up another set of emotions that had to be addressed independently.

As a group we had been through a traumatic event and we could not ignore that. We were feeling helpless in that we were not here for our colleague when she was attacked. The good news was that we were now here for each other and no one was left to manage this alone. Usually, in traumatic situations people tend to isolate themselves. Opening the lines of communication made a huge difference in managing this particular crisis.

To take things a step further, I arranged for the staff to have access to professionals off-site, but any additional support was beyond my scope. In the days to come, it was tough for all of us, but we did the *heavy lifting* as a group and individually. Some of the team sought out and participated in support groups. Facing our feelings head-on was important because we wanted to be able to take care of them in a way that helped us move forward.

After a while, I was back to my walk-throughs and normal engagements with the team and the residents. If not for any other reason than I needed to show the staff that it was possible to be effective in our respective roles while healing from the traumatic event.

Until one day … at eight months pregnant, I took a tumble down two steps. I don't know how I missed those steps, but I did. Someone heard the commotion in the stairway and came running to help me. I thought I could dust myself off and go to my office but no. They called the ambulance and I was rushed to the ER with elevated blood pressure and concerns for the health of my baby. Thankfully, the baby and I were ok, but my doctor was playing no games with me. I was a high-risk pregnancy, so I was not allowed to return to work. I spent the duration of my pregnancy on workers comp.

My doctor's restrictions turned out to be a blessing in disguise because following the fall were many aches and pains for which I could not be treated because I was pregnant. Once the baby was born, I would have several diagnostic tests done but still could not take any medication for the pain since I was breastfeeding.

Tests found that because of the fall I had torn a ligament in my knee that would ultimately land me in surgery. It was not the best news, but it was not the worst news either. You could imagine the *heavy lifting* that had to be done to manage the pain, deal with the emotions associated with being a new mom, and then undergo a surgery that would require months of physical therapy. There were periods of anxiety and hopelessness that I had to work through. I sought out professional mental health treatment because I needed to be mentally and emotionally healthy for me and my daughter. Many tears were shed, and many prayers went up because I honestly did not feel like I had the strength to be the mom and woman I knew I could be.

Months of struggle passed, but I put on a brave face so that those that loved me the most would not be worried about me. I did not want anyone to see the kink in my armor as I was always seen as "strong." How difficult is it to remove the veil of the perceptions of others and ask for help? Are you wearing a veil of strength while you are struggling in your cage experience? It's ok to ask for help. The longer you struggle in silence the longer you remain that caterpillar that can't transform. This is what happens when we feel like we are stuck.

The longer you struggle in silence the longer you remain that caterpillar that can't transform.

I would go on to spend the first full year of my daughter's life at home with her, being present for most of her first milestones. Though I was totally immersed in the fulfilment of motherhood, I wanted to get back to work, I was missing my life of service.

Along the way, I had decided that I would not be going back to the Institute for Community Living. The commute back and forth from Brooklyn to Queens was not what I wanted. As a new mom, my priorities were changing, I wanted to be able to get to my daughter quickly in case of an emergency.

Chapter 6

The Cage of Safety: A Safe Horizon

*"Safety is a basic human need. People with a sense
of security and belonging are stabilized for learning,
creating, innovating. A group of wonderfully cared for,
confident individuals will generate great ideas."*
— JOHN SWEENEY

We all want to be safe and free from harm, not just
feel safe, which is psychological. We create environments that make us feel safe. What do we do when we
discover that the safety net we thought we had is now
gone? After the experiences I had in previous work
environments, physical safety was now a priority.
Behind the wall, safety was inherent; the foundation,
after all, is safety and security. Yes, the threat of violence and gangs was ever present, but so were the
correctional officers. At the Institute for Community
Living, there were minimal safety precautions—until
the incident. I could no longer take for granted that
my work environment would be safe.

During my online search, I came across a job posting
for a Domestic Violence Shelter Director. Listen, I

knew that my credentials aligned but my experience with victims of domestic violence was limited but I was not afraid to work with yet another population that needed strong advocacy. I was interviewed and hired.

I showed up and was ready. In retrospect, I don't know what I was expecting that first day to be like. All I knew was that I landed a solid position, with a great salary, and the bonus was that it was within a ten-minute drive from my baby girl. ***VICTORY!***

I would spend the next couple of months learning a deeper level of empathy and understanding. We would receive distressing calls from women and children who just needed to get to a safe place. Though the women were in crisis, the shelter was a cage of physical safety. They did not have to worry about any physical attack on their lives in this space—economic, psychological, and spiritual safety would take a longer time to regain.

The shelter had constant intakes. My heart broke every time I saw a new resident come in battered and bruised with her children and whatever handful of her belongings she could manage. The safety that many of the women once felt with their partners was now gone and I was meeting them at a pivotal point in their cage experience. The point where they were acknowledging their abusive cage and were taking action.

TACTICAL PAUSE! If you are in a situation where your safety is compromised, there is help available. Please contact the National Domestic Violence Hotline at (800) 799-7233. At the Hotline, they safety plan with victims, friends, and family members—anyone who is concerned about their own safety or the safety of someone else. The safety plan will have all of the vital information you need and will be tailored to your unique situation. They will personally help walk you through different scenarios. The highest honor you could give yourself is getting to safety!

You may not know this, but when the women come into a shelter they are coming from another borough. That is an intentional part of the safety plan. The shelter is equipped to house and feed residents and their children. There is legal support available to help them navigate the court system and case managers that help the residents get set up with medical coverage and food benefits. Women are encouraged to secure gainful employment and supported in that search.

Establishing economic independence is a critical step in independence because the financial stronghold that some of these abusers have over the women causes them to stay or go back. On-site the shelter offers resume writing, mock interviewing; they also receive donations from Dress for Success, Baby Buggy, and Paul Mitchell, to name a few. Day care is also available for children that are not yet school aged. For those who are school aged, they help to get them set up in the local public school.

In this role, I was able to support these women through their *discovery* and *heavy lifting* phases and see them to the last phase: *VICTORY!*

The **VICTORY** Phase is one where we reflect on where we've come from and appreciate the hard work that was done to get this far. It is important to ac-knowledge the small wins as they can keep you moti-vated. This is not to say there is no more work to do, because there is. The **VICTORY!** here is that they made it out of the abusive situation they were in, but still the *heavy lifting* would be intense.

These women were trauma survivors who weren't feel-ing safe in their own bodies and certainly not in their relationships with others. They struggled with regu-

It is important to acknowledge the small wins as they can keep you motivated.

lating their everyday emotions, which they had asso-ciated directly with the trauma. It could take months or even years to regain a sense of safety. We provided the resources to support this journey to safety.

As I journeyed with the women, I did not always fully comprehend what they were feeling, but over time I learned it. This journey was not about me, it was about them, I had to learn how to be a resource to them. Bear with me, I was learning.

There was a point in their therapeutic process when they were mourning the end of their abusive relation-ships. I eventually grew to understand that this *heavy lifting* phase could be confusing. For some of them, the cage experience did not always hurt. Their abusers were sometimes nice, gentle, caring, compassionate, and complimentary. They missed that seemingly loving side of their abuser. Others reflected on the place of comfort that the abuser provided for them, big and beautiful homes for them and their children, until they did something that the abuser did not like, or thought was unacceptable. Trauma looked different for everyone that participated in the therapeutic sessions.

Can you think of situations that once made you feel safe and then one day the blanket got pulled from under you?

In those moments, you might stumble or even fall but you don't just stand there. These situations are temporary so you must regroup and recover. It may take some time for you to trust again but next time you will take control of your own safety and not give anyone the power to create that sense of instability in your life again. I know, we don't like to talk about these kinds of things, but you're not the only one.

I read of a French pioneering psychologist, Pierre Janet, who outlined what many believe is the first framework for trauma recovery in the late 1800s. In 1992, psychologist Judith Herman transformed Janet's initial ideas into a three-stage approach to understanding trauma.

Phase One: Safety and Stabilization. Trauma survivors tend to feel unsafe in their bodies and in relationships with others. They may struggle with regulating their everyday emotions, which they may not associate directly with the trauma. It may take months or even years to regain a sense of safety.

Phase Two: Remembrance and Mourning. This

is when survivors may begin to process the trauma, assigning words and emotions to it to help make meaning of it. This process is best undertaken with a trained counselor or therapist. It's important to mourn the losses associated with the trauma and give oneself space to grieve and express emotions.

Phase Three: Reconnection and Integration. Here, survivors recognize the impact of the victimization they experienced, yet begin to believe that trauma is no longer a defining principle in their life. They begin to redefine themselves in the context of meaningful relationships, create a new sense of self and create a new future. In some instances, they may find a mission through which they can heal and grow, such as mentoring or becoming an advocate for others.

This framework not only helped me to better support the women as they did the *heavy lifting* but continued to serve as a guide as I moved through my own cage experiences.

Many women really struggled with blaming themselves. Could they not see that they were further victimizing the victim? I had to understand that there was a conditioning process that they had been through and its effects could not be reversed overnight.

Have you been conditioned to accept your cage as the way, as something permanent?

I need you to know that while you are doing the *heavy lifting* to get free from your cage, the results will not come overnight but they *will* come.

You wanna know something?

I've got some more good news for you!

As long as you know that you are trapped or having a cage experience, you still have a chance to escape. Your cage experience can have a lifelong impact, but the severity of its effects can be lessened by getting help now.

It's Mary Holloway who said, "Resilience is knowing that you are the only one that has the power and the responsibility to pick yourself up." I witnessed true resiliency and the fighting spirit of women that brute force could not defeat. There were many times when I felt so hurt for them. I could not get used to hearing their stories of abuse. Every tear, every cut, every bruise, every excuse was a reminder of their cage and the pain suffered at the hand of an intimate partner. It was not ok.

I learned that sexual violence, stalking, and intimate partner violence are major public health problems in the United States. Many survivors of these forms of violence can experience physical injury; mental health consequences such as depression, anxiety, low self-esteem, and suicide attempts; and other health consequences such as gastrointestinal disorders, substance abuse, sexually transmitted diseases, and gynecological or pregnancy complications. These consequences can lead to hospitalization, disability, or death.

According to the National Intimate Partner and Sexual Violence Survey in 2010, more than one in three women (35.6 percent) and more than one in four men (28.5 percent) in the United States have experienced rape, physical violence, and/or stalking by an intimate partner in their lifetime.

Among victims of intimate partner violence, more than one in three women experienced multiple forms of rape, stalking, or physical violence; 92.1 percent of male victims experienced physical violence alone, and 6.3 percent experienced physical violence and stalking. Nearly one in ten women in the United States (9.4 percent) has been raped by an intimate partner in her lifetime, and an estimated 16.9 percent of women and 8.0 percent of men have experienced sexual violence other than rape by an intimate partner at some point in their lifetime. About one in four women (24.3 percent) and one in seven men (13.8 percent) have experienced severe physical violence by an intimate partner (e.g., hit with a fist or something hard, beaten, slammed against something) at some point in their lifetime.

An estimated 10.7 percent of women and 2.1 percent of men have been stalked by an intimate partner during their lifetime. Nearly half of all women and men in the United States have experienced psychological aggression by an intimate partner in their lifetime (48.4 percent and 48.8 percent, respectively).

Furthermore, most female and male victims of rape, physical violence, and/or stalking by an intimate partner (69 percent of female victims; 53 percent of male victims) experienced some form of intimate partner violence for the first time before twenty-five years of age.

The magnitude of this cage is remarkable, and the **heavy lifting** requires professional support. I would not recommend anyone go at this alone.

I experienced more vicarious trauma in my three months there than I had experienced in prison in a decade. For those of you who may not be familiar with the term, vicarious trauma is the emotional residue of exposure that counselors have from working with people as they hear their trauma stories and become witnesses to the pain, fear, and terror that trauma survivors have endured. Those with vicarious trauma are at risk of developing mental health issues because they might neglect their own issues. These issues may include anxiety, clinical depression, post-traumatic stress disorder, and addiction, among other problems. Therefore, it is important to address this trauma as soon as possible.

While the team never complained of experiencing vicarious trauma, through everyday conversations with them, many of them mentioned having signs and symptoms that I knew were associated with the work they were doing. Perhaps they were too close to the work to realize it. I decided that having professionals come in to do some team building, resiliency training, and trauma-centered in-service couldn't hurt.

The initiative was received well by my Vice President and the staff, but I have to say, the effort wasn't as selfless as I'd like people to think. I, too, needed to learn how to take care of my mind and body. I was absolutely drowning in empathy, so much so that my body stopped lactating for my daughter despite my pumping efforts.

When you are in the business of service it is easy to get lost in the work. There are so many people that need support out there.

As a servant leader you tend to intuitively put the needs of your employees first. I knew that they would be no good to themselves, the residents, or the business if they became emotionally or psychologically over-whelmed. I understood the broader implications if awareness was not raised and support was not offered.

Additionally, because trust is so important with this population, I did not want to start seeing staff turnover. It can be very challenging re-establishing those trusting therapeutic relationships. Somehow, I knew that proactively addressing our self-care needs would be in the best interest of all parties. Research shows that doctors, nurses, personal support workers, counselors, therapists, social workers, police officers, soldiers, rescue workers and the like are particularly susceptible to this trauma experience.

The people I worked with were amazing, they had such beautiful souls; some were a little cynical, but the experience was worth it. The work was good. The commute was great. My light was dimming and the weight of the abuse of others became too heavy to carry. Compassion fatigue was not something I was particularly familiar with at the time, but as I write this book now, it is clear to me. I started thinking that something was wrong with me, that I just could not unhear the stories nor could I unsee the bruises. Doing that would require more than I could give at the time.

Here I was, helping to heal others while neglecting my own hurt. Admittedly, that was a bit easier. Working in this setting forced me to look at myself and be honest with what I was personally dealing with, a failing marriage. With compassion fatigue setting in, I did not have the energy required to do the ***heavy lifting***, but I knew I would have to. I could no longer avoid this.

Though my husband was not the possessive type, my marriage was a cage. I wanted it to work. I didn't want to fail at it. I grew up with parents who are still married, almost fifty years later. And, almost on cue, in comes the influence of the reliable Familial Cage. I wanted my daughter to grow up in a home with her mom and dad, but I could not live unhappily. Yes, I am ready to let you all in and talk about my own hurt.

Professionally, I felt like a rock star. I knew I was good to my people and I was great for business. I had always respected the power of soft skills, so I took every available opportunity to truly develop them and the return on that time invested, to this day, is solid. Personally, I thought I was doing all the "right" things, including pre-marital counseling.

At this time in my life, I was newly married to a man that represented everything safe for me and our brand-new daughter. I met him at church. In my eyes, he was everything. He promised to be a provider, a protector, a great husband, and a great dad. He had met with my parents and promised them that their daughter would never want for anything. Though my parents were not impressed, they took him at his word and asked me if this was something I was sure I wanted to do. Of course, love had me blinded, so I said, "Yes."

FYI, not one promise was kept.

Though his heart may have been in the right place, he completely misrepresented himself. Perhaps he overestimated what he thought he was realistically capable of. For the sake of transparency, unbeknownst to me, he had many of his own traumas and demons to deal with.

While my husband was not abusive toward me, it was not a healthy home environment. In my heart of hearts, I know that he loved us, but he was not ready for what a true partnership would require. I was also not ready for the *heavy lifting* that would be required to free myself from this cage.

Sometimes the amount of unpacking to be done to get to the root cause can be grueling.

Sometimes the amount of unpacking to be done to get to the root cause can be grueling.

You may want to zip your baggage back up and put it in a corner for another time. But what does that really do for you? Nothing. No one else can unpack your baggage and do the necessary sorting.

I had to acknowledge that this situation was not healthy for any of us, regardless of how I wished and prayed for it to be. I, too, had to prepare for my dream of happily ever after to no longer exist. I had to consider what this would mean for my daughter. I had to have some very sensitive conversations with my husband who didn't see my perspective and couldn't understand where I was coming from. His inability to accept my truth did not change the way I was feeling. At this point, I was not seeking his validation of my feelings. I wanted us to all be genuinely happy and this was not it.

To me, this was a personal failure. I had to go back to my family and let them know it was not working and that I had made the decision to walk away. The last thing I wanted or needed to hear was "we told you so." I did not hear that. My parents just asked me what I needed. I did not know what I needed; I'd have to figure it out.

I recommend the following steps as you navigate your cage experiences as it has consistently worked for me:

1. Adjust **your** depth of focus

2. Create the mental distance **you** need

3. Tap into the social intelligence **you've** developed

4. Create a plan that leverages **your** practical intelligence

This process is all about **you**. As life gets difficult, remember that **you** are transforming. No one else can transform for **you** because that transformation comes from the inside out.

For me, instead of focusing on the marriage and all the variables I personally had no control over, I focused on being happy as a person and as a mom, I had someone to be successful for.

As Barack Obama says, "Find someone to be successful for. Raise their hopes. Rise to their needs." Even if I did not want to do this for myself, I knew that my daughter needed healthy parents and needed to grow up in a home filled with love, not one of unhappiness and discord.

Going to work every day was one way I created the mental distance I needed but know that I truly just wanted to pull the covers over my head and not deal at all.

The other way I created distance was moving out. It was so hard to come to terms with this decision because I knew couples rarely bounced back from this level of separation, especially newlyweds. With much trepidation, I moved out. I needed to be out of the environment to gain some clarity of thought. If we were going to be able to work things out in the future or at least be agreeable co-parents, the distance was a necessity.

Social intelligence was all that I had learned to this point. The offenders behind the wall taught me of the hurt, pain, and plight of the black man. My time with the women in the shelter broadened my perspectives on life and relationships. Their fire gave me the courage I needed to take the next step. I had formulated my plan.

When I coach my people, I would always say, just take one step. One successful step builds confidence, the next step builds more confidence, and so on. Soon, your motivation will be fueled by all the successful steps that **YOU** have made. You will have proven to yourself that you can successfully walk alone.

One successful step builds confidence, the next step builds more confidence, and so on. Soon, your motivation will be fueled by all the successful steps that YOU have made.

Being able to put my shelter experience in my rear-view for a while was great, but little did I know, I would soon encounter this population again. This time, they would be behind the wall—that good ole Cage of Comfort rearing its head again.

Chapter 7

The Professional Cage: Prison Administrator

"Most people chase success at work, thinking that will make them happy. The truth is that happiness at work will make you successful."

— ALEXANDER KJERULF

Don't you just love your job? Yes, you're loving it? No, looking for your next opportunity? Wherever you fall on the spectrum, just know that you have plenty of company there. Many of us find joy, fulfillment, and purpose in our careers. We work long hours to meet our commitments, while sacrificing other unacknowledged areas of our lives.

In Corrections, I've seen folks work hours and hours of voluntary overtime. If it's available, they're making the money. Period. Side note, that this is different from the mandatory overtime that is driven by the staffing challenges in the facilities throughout the nation.

Working as a Prison Health Services Administrator came with its challenges, but it was extremely rewarding. The work was meaningful, and the population was appreciative. Admittedly, I did not always want to be identified as the "Administrator" because Constantine Alleyne was a person who had feelings. The Administrator had to make tough decisions that did not always align with Constantine Alleyne the person. There were many times when my staff and the offender population could not separate the two.

Following through with the directives from senior leadership was not always popular, especially with my understanding of the impact many of those directives would have on the staff. Who cared about that? I had a job to do and expectations to meet. Regardless of how tactful I was, it would not change the outcome.

The Professional Cage is an unavoidable cage because most of us spend more time in our work environments than we spend in our home environments.

The Professional Cage is an unavoidable cage because most of us spend more time in our work environments than we spend in our home environments.

Just think of how much time we put in to make it to retirement. I'm not sure who wants to spend the majority of their lives professionally miserable? I don't. Let's face it, this cage is quite formidable. You, me, we are tougher!

There is nothing like working with the female offender population. See, the bulk of my experience behind the wall was with men. I may have supported the efforts in a female facility in the past, but it was never my sole responsibility. At this point in my career, I had now worked with just about every demographic I could have ever wanted to work with. I had worked with corporate sharks on Wall Street, the geriatric population at the nursing home, female victims, the male offenders on Rikers Island (which included the criminal element, mentally ill, medically compromised, homeless, substance abusers, etc.), and now the female offender.

You might be wondering how I got here. Let me rewind... I knew that I had to leave the shelter, so I decided to see what was out there. Following a visit to a longtime friend, I decided Connecticut would be my landing place. I could see, in that very moment, the life I wanted for me and my daughter. Certainly, I needed to make sure I had a job and that I could establish a healthy home environment for my daughter. So, I looked for a job and got hired. I don't know if it was good fortune, my ancestors, the universe, or God, or maybe it was just that the stars had aligned but relocating anywhere is never an easy decision. You are leaving a piece of your life behind and you must deal with the relative mixed emotions.

The University of Connecticut had a posting out there for a Health Services Administrator II. They held the contract for Correctional Health Care. I went through a few rounds of interviewing and the job was mine. I was told they were impressed with my vast experience with different populations and within different environments. Additionally, my fellow Administrators were happy to know that I had experience working in a unionized environment. I must say I was very happy to have been able to secure a role with such a sound organization, with a pretty decent salary.

For some reason, I feel like this is really where my story begins. Little did I know, this is where I would see the culmination of what I was made of finally come to life. Aside from going into a female facility, which I will dive deeper into later, I was stepping into the role of single, working mom. I never knew how hard that role would be. The struggle would be real! And, of course, I could not keep it simple, I added a puppy and an Executive MBA to the mix. Life was laughable!

Much more **heavy lifting**! The emotions I had to manage were much more than I had anticipated. It wasn't just me managing me. Now I would have no support and needed to figure out how to truly manage my time.

My two paths of growth were not mutually exclusive. I had to figure out how to be a single mom and still feed my ambitions.

My two paths of growth were not mutually exclusive. I had to figure out how to be a single mom and still feed my ambitions. For the first six months of employment, I commuted back and forth from New York City to Hartford, Connecticut. I had given up my apartment and moved back home with my parents. I would wake up at 4 a.m., leave home by 5 a.m. to get to work before 8 a.m. I knew if I had left any later, I would encounter so much traffic on I-95 and I-91. I would leave Connecticut at 4 p.m. or 5 p.m. and sit in the traffic going home. Lord knows it was a tiring day; I would arrive back in Brooklyn exhausted. On a few days, I would pull into a rest stop for a couple moments of sleep. I knew that when I got home, my now eighteen-month-old would be looking for playtime or bonding time with her mom.

I could see the life I wanted. Determination, not fear, was in the driver seat taking us there.

My goal was to save enough money for a down payment on a home. I did not want to move my daughter ever again.

Here's the thing, while my personal life was stabilizing, my professional life was soaring. I stepped into the facility in Hartford and was received well by the staff. They had an appreciation for my leadership style, and we worked quite well together. The facility was all men, so I was definitely in my comfort zone. And what happens?? I get a call from my central office stating that they would like to talk with me about a sensitive matter. Turns out, I was being reassigned.

This is life, though. Change happens. Just when you think you've got it all figured out; you get thrown for a loop. Ok, ok. It made me stumble but not fall. I had to regroup and figure some things out to make this work. Could I have looked for another job? Sure, but I was there to work in Corrections, not to just find some other random job that did not align with my purpose.

I did what I always do. I walked in with confidence, like I was supposed to be there. Truth be told, I had no idea where I was going nor what I was supposed to be doing. The Administrator came out, met me on the walkway, and escorted me to what would become my office in a little more than a week. It was clear in our first interactions that he was not fond of me. As far as he knew, I was there to take his job and he was not going to make it easy for me.

Here is the thing about God, He doesn't put you in places and spaces that he has not prepared you for. Psalms 23:5 says: "Thou preparest a table before me in the presence of mine enemies: thou anointest my head with oil; my cup runneth over." I knew I was on assignment and there was nothing this dude could have done to throw me off course. Yes, it was discouraging but the desire to be liked was never a strong one of mine. I would discover that the women behind the wall needed an advocate, and one that looked like them.

As I familiarized myself with the civilian staff, I became familiar with the custody staff, a much more difficult dance. Another thing that it would be important to mention here is that I was just one of three African American women in leadership at this facility. Unlike Hartford, where the workforce was multicultural, this facility was down by the shore, where most of the staff were Caucasian. The reason I think this is important to mention here is because race had never been an issue for me behind the wall.

In NYC, the workforce was diverse, race was a non–issue. However, I would find there to be some officers who took issue with the richness of my melanin and would try to use it against me. The *heavy lifting* associated with handling this workplaces' microaggressions would require more than just this chapter.

One of the offenders who had work detail in my area, came to me and said, "Ms. Connie, you know they put up a memo in the units that said they will only issue us two tampons and two pads?' In my mind, I thought this could not be true. Who would do such a thing? Was there some new protocol or guideline that I was unaware of? Was the budgetary constraint this bad that we would open the population up to infections? So, I asked the offender if she could get the letter for me so I could have a conversation with my Clinic Captain, in keeping with the chain of command, Nursing Supervisor, and my Women's Health APRN.

As a woman, I could not imagine going through my menstrual cycle only using two tampons and two pads. From a clinical perspective, this is not appropriate hygienic practice for vaginal health nor mental health. On a broader scale, considering the odors that would start ruminating, we could be opening ourselves up to all kinds of hostilities amongst the population. This was wrong on so many levels.

Turns out that the Clinic Captain was not aware of any changed protocols and did not know where this memorandum had come from. He listened to our perspectives from a Health Services lens and asked that I accompany him to the Warden's office. I had such an appreciation for his immediate attention to this matter and for the fact that he knew it needed to be escalated.

We arrived at the Warden's office and learned that, apparently, he did not authorize this memo either, but now it was a topic for discussion. In the meantime, the memos were taken down from across the compound, but we were told we would discuss this further at the Warden's meeting the next day.

The next day, I walked into the Warden's meeting to a sea of blue uniforms and male, Caucasian faces. Perhaps I should have been intimidated, but I wasn't. He went through the items of the agenda and arrived at Medical.

It was my turn.

I introduced myself as I hadn't seen many of those faces before and I produced copies of the memo so that everyone in the room would know what I was referencing. I proceeded.

First, it was important to me to identify the author as he or she may have some information that I simply did not have. Next, I decided to educate the room on vaginal health and explained that when we weigh the expense of tampons and pads with the cost of medication, surgeries, and adding more medical providers to the head count, we would not be saving but assuming heftier burdens on already strained budgets. While I thought the point was made, there was one who said, "Who gives a shit? Let them buy their own stuff from commissary!"

Firstly, who talks like this in an official meeting? Secondly, are we in the twilight zone? Is this acceptable here? Clearly, this individual did not know the population that he was serving.

I said, "Officer, as we all know, this population rarely has any money in their commissary and would not be able to meet this need long-term. As it stands, their dietary needs go unmet, so they buy food with the little funds they have. To add insult to injury, they pay a high price to make phone calls to their families. They also pay for sick calls when they are not well. I am not here to educate you about the impact of mass incarceration or give any lessons on the economics of prison and jail, I'm here this morning to make sure that the health care needs of the population are being adequately met."

The room was silent. The Warden said, "Connie, I understand your point and we will discard the unauthorized memo."

I simply said, "Thank you." I was pleased with the outcome. **_VICTORY!_**

The meeting went on as usual, but it was when the meeting ended that the chatter began. Someone said, "You know if she didn't look like them, she wouldn't be in here advocating."

I don't know if it was the "**_them_**" or the attack on my character that got to me. I had developed such a thick skin on my journey, and I tried to maintain my professional demeanor because I did not want to fall into that angry black woman stereotype. However, I turned and said, "Many of them look like you and your mother and your sister and your aunties! They are human beings and I am here to advocate for us treating them as such; they're already being punished for their crime."

This was just one of quite a few racially driven experiences I had there. The worst had to be the day I was walking down the corridor, in a pair of navy slacks, a maroon blouse that had a loose bow tied at the collar, and a pair of navy-blue low pumps. A Caucasian officer stops me and says, "Show me your ID."

I was confused, "I said, excuse me?"

He said, "Show me your ID."

"Why are you asking for my ID?" I asked. "Have you asked every other employee you've passed for their ID?"

"There was an escape and the colors you are wearing are close to inmate colors."

I said, "Officer, you know that I am not an inmate. I think it would be in your best interest to keep moving as I head down to the Warden's office to discuss this exchange."

He said, "Now why would you do that?"

I did not answer, I showed him my employee identification card with my name and title and moved on. As I was walking, he followed, apologizing for his "mistake."

This was no mistake; he knew what he was doing. He just did not know who I was and that there would be consequences for his actions. This microaggression was a negative prejudicial slight that I could not take lightly. It was tough being a woman in Corrections and even tougher being a Black woman in a position of authority in Corrections.

Granted, my authority was within the confines of the compound, but it needs to be understood that the power struggle is real behind the wall. Those who don't have it, want it, and those who have it, don't want to lose it. I found that to be true within the offender subculture and amongst the employees; making it critical that you understand the chain of command.

At the peak of staffing, I had about (130) direct reports that included medical doctors, psychiatrists, psychologists, social workers, APRNs. RNs, LPNs, dentists, dental assistants, clerical support staff, an X-ray tech, and a phlebotomist. I was expected to know what was going on at all times and to come up with solutions to the issues that arose. I got to know all of the staff and was intentional about coming in on all shifts so they were not just an employee number to me but my teammates who had their own goals and objectives. I made the effort to cultivate those working relationships. I never wanted any of the team to feel irrelevant or less valued, especially my night shift warriors.

It took me some time to have a 1:1 with each staff member, but I did it. That was something that was important to me. Also, when I was in the facility, I was visible to the offender population, my team, and custody.

The weight of over (130) direct reports was more than I realized it would be. I was orienting, coaching, and mentoring these employees and they trusted me to guide them through their careers. I had an open-door policy and made myself available. Certainly, there were times where appointments were needed as I had tasks and priorities I had to achieve as well. My open-door policy was the gateway to free-flowing information. There was very little I did not know was happening in the facility. My team would call me all hours of the day and night to let me know what was going on. My Warden would call all hours of the day and night to let me know of any matters of concern that arose on the custody side of the house, such as things that were going on in the units that could ultimately impact service provision.

The Offenders. This was a different kind of **heavy lifting**. Have you ever carried a load that was not your own? Someone else's trauma? Their hurts? Their disappointments?

Here's the good news, it's not yours! You can choose to lay that load down.

While these women were certainly not all innocent; they were not all guilty either. Many of them were broken in ways I could not easily grasp. The lives they reported to have led were similar to those you might see in an Investigation Discovery documentary.

I would frequently go to some of my social workers' groups to get to know their clinical styles and get to know the population a bit. The vast majority of women are in jail for nonviolent offenses—32 percent for property offenses, 29 percent for drug offenses, and 21 percent for public order offenses. Of jailed women, 82 percent report a history of drug or alcohol abuse or dependency.

According to the Federal Bureau of Prisons, women account for approximately 7 percent of the Federal inmate population. Nationwide, women are a growing correctional population; however, in the Bureau of Prisons, women have maintained a steady proportion of the overall population. The Bureau houses women in twenty-nine facilities across the country.

Women in Bureau custody are offered many of the same educational and treatment programs that are available to male offenders; however, women in prison differ from their male counterparts in significant ways. For example, women are more likely to experience economic hardship, employment instability, and fewer vocational skills as compared with males. Women are more likely than men to have a history of trauma and abuse, which poses additional challenges for re-entry, specialized initiatives, and programs that are trauma-informed and address women's gender-based needs.

The needs of women in prison are very different than those of men. Many women are the caregivers for their children. Though they lose their freedom, they don't all lose their parental rights. I had a front row seat to the system trying to justify the rights of mothers. For those of you who may not know this, not all systems allow for women who give birth to keep their children behind the wall with them. Most systems do not have the infrastructure to support the needs of an infant, so women who give birth are allowed to bond with their newborn for the couple of days they are in the hospital and then the baby goes to the father or next of kin. In cases where there is no father or next of kin willing to take custody of the baby, the baby can become a ward of the state.

For those women who want to breastfeed, they are allowed to breastfeed while in the hospital and then given the permission to pump and store their milk while living in the medical infirmary. There was significant opposition to this practice.

One argument was that once you come to prison, you lose the right to breastfeed, so the facility should not be forced to make special accommodations for the mother. Another argument involved chain of custody of the breast milk and the liability that the Department of Correction would have if the infant got sick from the milk.

Although Custody could not see the possibilities, we made an outline of every single possibility in order for the women to gain favorable consideration for their right to feed their babies. First, we brought forth the conversation about the women not losing their parental rights just because they are incarcerated nor did they lose their right to choose. Though Custody would have liked to control the dialogue they could not unilaterally decide that pumping and storing milk would create any safety and security concerns.

This decision involved us considering women's rights, inmate rights, and human rights. We highlighted that our local hospital was willing to donate an industrial pump that could be used in the medical infirmary where the breast milk would be labeled and frozen. The resistance to a compromise was palpable but we needed a solution that did not violate the rights of the population and one that would mitigate our liabilities. There were solutions, we just needed to come to an agreement. Almost two weeks later, an agreement was reached but not without much agita.

The women who chose to pump and dump or pump and store would have to live in the infirmary during that time. It was not the best solution. Women pumping milk should not have to live in an infirmary setting because they were not sick, they were pumping milk. Infirmary beds were a hot commodity because open beds were limited and needed for medically ill patients, not healthy mothers who just wanted to pump and send milk home to their babies.

This is one of those times where Custody simply did not want the women to have this right and we were not going to get this win easily. An important thing to note here is that when you are housed in the infirmary, you do not have the same access to programming and other support services. Essentially, they wanted mothers to choose between breastfeeding and personal development.

There was no way I would allow that.

I had received a call from a lactation advocate from Yale New Haven Hospital who suddenly wanted to speak to me about the women breast pumping and feeding. It turns out that one of our high-risk pregnancy offenders was receiving prenatal care there and expressed her concern about what would possibly happen once she delivered. I did not want to, in any way, compromise this offender, so I did not bring her pregnancy or treatment into the ongoing debate with Custody. I did let Custody leadership know we now had advocates inquiring, which I believe motivated them to be a bit more progressive in their thinking and to stop trying to impose any undue punishment on the women.

Every effort was always made to avoid negative publicity, so I thought we had turned the corner. But still someone came up with one of the most absurd arguments. As if this debate could get any more ridiculous, this individual suggested that if we allowed the women to freeze their breast milk, they will use it as a weapon.

Perhaps you have heard of death by breast milk? No? Me either.

If ever there was a waste of taxpayer dollars, the number of hours we spent in meetings about this could have funded the purchase of a couple of breast pumps.

Finally, we came to the agreement to allow the women to pump and dump or pump and store. Once they've pumped, the nurses would label and store the milk in the freezer. When the next of kin comes to the facility to pick up the milk, the nurse would give the package of frozen breast milk to the officer who would escort the offender to the visiting area to give the package to the next of kin. This exchange was only authorized to happen on the days that the offender was scheduled to have a visit.

During this time, I'd learned to work within the limits I had, as well as to push them a bit. I know that the Warden would not have wanted the Yale advocate coming in and interviewing their patients—his inmates. One thing is for sure, he did not need any negative press. No facility wants the press at their front door. I understood that having outsiders coming to our door was a last resort and we would do our best to avoid that from happening.

Now, the professional in me was sure to return the call of the Yale advocate and inform her of the agreement that we came to, ensuring that offender rights were not being infringed upon. Thankfully that conversation satisfied the inquiry. This situation reminded me that when you align with your purpose the work does not feel like a burden. You are where you are supposed to be, doing what you are supposed to be doing. During another unlikely encounter I was served another healthy dose of purpose.

I recall during one of my group visits, there were five offenders in the room as well as the social worker, and one of the offenders looked over at me, and said, "Who are you?"

I replied, "I am the Administrator. I am just here to observe and if there is anything of value I could offer, I will." I wasn't sure what to expect from this woman.

She looked me up and down, and said, "Oh shit! You Black. They ain't ever had no Black administrator in charge of all these white people!"

I looked at her, and said, "I am happy to be here with y'all."

I thought that would have been enough, but the offender continued. She said," Miss, do you realize that you being here is going to give a lot of us hope? You must be really smart, too. Can you tell us your story?"

You may not know why you are in a particular space or place, but your impact may ripple far beyond your intentions.

It was not my intention to disrupt the therapeutic process, so I looked at my social worker for guidance on how she wanted to proceed. She asked that I tell them my story, so I did. When the session was over a few women were in tears and others congratulated me on my new role. My social worker and I talked after about the power in the offender's words and that somehow my very presence as a Black woman was serving as motivation to some. Those words have been with me since.

You may not know why you are in a particular space or place, but your impact may ripple far beyond your intentions.

My journey taught me compassion and empathy. I learned how to use my voice in a way that was effective. I learned to navigate crucial conversations without being threatening nor acquiescing. I was what the women needed. I was what this system needed.

My advocacy did not stop in the facility. I joined the Policy and Procedure Committee, where I was able to use all of my public health insights and correctional experiences to influence policy changes for populations who could not advocate for themselves. This was a full circle moment for me and my greatest personal achievement. I was actively influencing policies that would allow the offender population to live behind the wall with dignity.

I am reminded of this TED Talk I once saw. It was called "The Danger of the Single Story," by Chimamanda Ngozi Adichie. She is a Nigerian woman who is reflecting on her stories. If I hadn't worked in the U.S. prisons and jails and all I knew about offenders were from the popular images seen on television, I, too, would think that all offenders were unfeeling, uneducated, manipulative, low income crooks incapable of being productive members of society.

Offenders have been shown as one thing, as only one thing, over and over again and that is what they have become in the eyes of the masses. We have not taken the time to engage with the true stories of these offenders. I couldn't agree more with Chimamanda's view on the consequences of a single story, it robs individuals of their dignity and it makes our recognition of our equal humanity difficult. Our limited exposure to their stories has been used to dispossess and to malign. Stories can break the dignity of people, but stories can also repair that broken dignity. Knowing I was a part of the healing process was confirmation that I was walking in my purpose.

I would go on to serve on the Policy and Procedure Committee for the duration of my time in the system. I successfully led the reaccreditation activities for National Commission on Correctional Health Care and the NCCHC Opioid Treatment Program.

In 2015, I was selected as a Connecticut Health Foundation Leadership Fellow. I learned more about health equity and the drivers for negative health outcomes based on race and socioeconomic status. This training opened my eyes to other ways I could serve. The combination of work experience, training, and my advanced degrees only confirmed that I was capable of more.

When I reflected on what had become a life of service, I realized that helping people, connecting to people, was something that I did naturally. Fifteen years in Corrections and I was ready to be free of that cage.

I decided that I would take everything I learned about Corrections and give it back to the industry. My gift back came in the form of the Civilian Corrections Academy.

"Twenty and done." Yes, that's the motto. Correctional professionals start their careers and retire at the twenty-year mark, leaving the industry and taking all of that invaluable experience with them. If that is you, you need to know that it does not have to be the end. You can use your experiences to help those just coming into the industry. Your departure from the industry only increases the tilt away from safe and stable environments, leaving your brothers and sisters at risk.

I decided that I would take everything I learned about Corrections and give it back to the industry. My gift back came in the form of the Civilian Corrections Academy.

For you, my reader, who is not in Corrections, it is important that you know the value you hold. Your years of on-the-job training and professional development can be put to great use if you so choose. Your intellectual property is critical to someone else's success. What is your give back? There's someone out there wishing they knew what you know.

There is no need for you to fall back into your Cage of Comfort when you can help someone else navigate their Cage of Innocence.

Part IV: VICTORY!

Chapter 8

Civilian Corrections Academy

"It is better to conquer yourself than to win in a thousand battles. The victory is yours. It cannot be taken from you, not by angels or by demons, heaven or hell."

— Buddha

Let's talk about fear, it always makes the Cage of Comfort look so appealing. Doing the podcast was one thing but putting myself out there as an expert in the Corrections space, as a Founder of anything, and as a Professor was another. I created a civilian path where there was none. I was telling the industry that there was a deficiency in their process. It definitely crossed my mind that if this was what I was supposed to be doing I wouldn't be so afraid. I told myself that I was afraid because I was not ready. Yeah, I know … more negative self-talk.

On the other hand, I reflect on a quote that I'd read that said, "If your dream doesn't scare you then you are not dreaming big enough." I was sufficiently freaked out! But really, I could interview drug dealers, murderers, and rapists, but I couldn't train others? I was too scared to write a book? Go figure.

Business school had laid the foundation and now I had to become the architect of my future. I researched all day and night. I had to find people that I could talk to about the process of building a viable business and working for oneself because it was unfamiliar territory. I was good at working for someone else. It felt great having a paycheck being directly deposited every two weeks.

Was I ready or willing to give that "sense" of security up?

I say sense because I've learned enough through the years to know that you can be relieved of your duties at any given moment, the majority of us are "at will employees." The moment you cease to produce, or you no longer meet the need of your employer, they will make the decision that letting you go is in their best interest. I had no way of knowing how long it was going to take to create this masterpiece. I can say masterpiece now, but it felt like I was walking down a pitch-black corridor and all I could do is feel for the walls to guide me to the light. I tapped into all of the available resources I could for guidance. Truth be told, I didn't even know I had a masterpiece inside me. I knew Corrections!

What I also knew was that I wanted to continue to serve the industry that I'd grown to love. I had to come to terms with the level of comfort I had working behind the wall and the discomfort I had in the entrepreneurial arena. It was not easy narrowing down my sea of thoughts because they were scattered, and I was intimidated but finally, I got there. ***VICTORY!***

I decided that there were tons of information and resources available to correctional officers but little to nothing available to the civilian workforce. I had a relatively successful career in Corrections, but how could I help other non-uniformed employees do the same?

Now, let's not gloss over the fact that you have the same opportunity here. As you examine your mental rolodex of challenges in your industry, can you think of some practical solutions?

That's the thing, we tend to overcomplicate matters when we don't have to. No one says that you have to have all of the answers. What you can do, is critically think about all of the workarounds you've created in order to get your job done. When you leave your role, no one will know what you were doing to be so efficient. You can take that knowledge and focus your efforts to create a business solution for your industry.

Now, let's not gloss over the fact that you have the same opportunity here. As you examine your mental rolodex of challenges in your industry, can you think of some practical solutions?

The Civilian Corrections Academy would be my solution, the one stop shop for civilian employees. I would offer mentoring, coaching, and training. My non-threatening disposition made it easy for others to take me under their wing and for others to want me to take them under my wing. Whether you are in Corrections or not, an abrasive disposition will close more doors than it will open. As you move through this world, it will matter how you present yourself and how you treat people. I can now say that Corrections was where I needed to be.

I did not know anything about the criminal element of the world or much about the social issues that plagued our society and filled the prison pipeline, but I wanted to learn.

Formal and informal mentor/mentee relationships can change the trajectory of your career. Many seasoned officers and civilian staff served as my mentors. They taught me things about the job that I could not learn from any textbook. They taught me lessons I would have gotten hurt by if I had learned them first-hand.

Though you may not be in the early stages of your professional life cycle, you have to remain coachable. Are you?

Having a mentor or coach is great and it worked well for me, but I saw vulnerabilities that I would share, and they would get lumped into the "that's how it always was and how we always do it" bucket. Whatever you do, please don't allow anyone to minimize your ideas because they are stuck in the past. Not everyone has your vision nor should they.

My reality is that what I felt the civilian workforce needed transcended my ability to put it into words. I needed to somehow capture my evolution and my mental transformation. Continuing to work in Corrections would not afford me the depth of focus and mental distance that I would need to think and reflect.

So, what did I do? I decided to leave Corrections and enter a completely different industry. *VICTORY!*

I took all of my transferable skills and stepped into the world of commercial and military engines.

Yes, you heard me correctly. I took on a role as a Service Contracts and Warranty Manager, where I managed the operator relationship throughout an engine's lifecycle. Yes, I had to learn about the gear turbofan and commercial engines. I know more about main gearboxes, fan blades, and piston seals than I'd like to, but I completely immersed myself in my role. I learned the business and how to maneuver. I helped develop best practices and standard work. I served as lead on a small team developing a contract management tool that did not exist. I also led initiatives related to the employee experience for remote and international employees.

I was doing meaningful work, but Corrections had my heart.

Now, I know I'm not the only one with a "side hustle" that has the potential to replace your full-time job.

After work I would go home, disconnect from commercial engines and lock into a narrow chamber of thought. I would explore my mental landscape for the keys to civilian success.

Now, I know I'm not the only one with a "side hustle" that has the potential to replace your full-time job. I'm not just talking about a passion project that won't matter next month. Finally, I began to carve out a path for me to lay the foundation. ***VICTORY!***

Civilian Corrections Academy provides the civilian workforce with key insights into the correctional environment. We serve as an added layer of protection to what the traditional training academy is providing.

I had identified a vulnerability in the industry and spent the next six months collecting the evidence needed to either support or redirect my path forward. While most systems make best efforts to provide training to all employees, I knew first-hand that the training needs of an officer were very different than those of a civilian. Specifically, civilians need to have a comprehensive understanding of the rules of engagement. The way you engage a patient in the community is very different from the way you engage an offender. The way you engage with someone in a traditional work environment is different from the way you engage correctional staff.

This is not necessarily to say that your engagements would be less professional. Instead, you would need to learn their language and talk to them from the lens that guides their actions. Knowing the directives, policies, procedures, and post orders will make all the difference in being able to achieve your mission.

A true examination of individual personality traits that offenders may target and attempt to exploit through their manipulative behaviors would be the next area of focus. What I found was that professional boundaries are easily crossed when employees don't understand ways in which they are vulnerable. Offenders take the time to learn our vulnerabilities, so we need to be steps ahead of them. For example, I knew I had a soft heart for women who were victims of abuse. I knew that my bias could possibly cloud my judgment so when offenders would write letters to my office expressing the need for support services, I would pass it on to one of the members of the clinical team instead of personally seeing it through. It can be difficult developing the social intelligence you need behind the wall, but my goal is to help develop that.

Over the years, I have developed disciplines through challenging encounters and visual cues from the subtlest of signs. Hand movements, eye movement, slight shifts in the body, etc. are all things that civilians need to be mindful of as they have their encounters with the offender population. Through the academy, we highlight the importance of remaining vigilant and aware of your environment, diving into situational awareness, environmental awareness, and physical awareness.

One place I've seen civilians truly miss the opportunity to serve as a partner to D.O.C. is that we don't put in the effort to understand their mission and vision for the department. We come into the facility nervous and decide we are going to just do what we do best, and that is our jobs. However, the level of interdependence on each other to do our jobs can't be ignored. As a service provider, you won't see any of your people if not for the officer ensuring that the offenders make it to your workspace. It is vital that we increase our understanding of and alignment with the D.O.C. mission and vision.

This is no easy task, especially if you work for a third party/a vendor. You will have to balance the demands that are within the scope of your role with the agenda of your organization and D.O.C. There will be more times than not where they will all be in conflict with each other. The decisions you make in those moments could make or break your career and certainly many professional relationships you might have established. Through the Academy, we focus on building cross-functional teams. The ***Alleyne & Co. Cross-Functional Engagement Model*** was developed as a framework for which both custody and civilians can work together seamlessly.

VICTORY!

The Alleyne & Co. Cross-Functional

Engagement Model

The main goals of cross-functional engagement are development, efficiency, transformation, and alignment. The ***Alleyne & Co Cross-Functional Engagement Model*** has proven to get us there.

What we know is that engagement is the difference between an employee who just does enough to get by and an employee who always goes the extra mile. In Corrections, the stakes are very high; we are navigating work related dangers, institutional dangers, and psychological dangers. We cannot afford to not have all eyes and ears at attention, contributing to the collective intelligence.

Because this is such an important point, I want to break it down a bit further so we all are clear on what I mean.

Work related dangers: staff assaults, infectious disease (like COVID-19), security risk groups (gangs), contraband, the offenders, and augmentations.

Institutional dangers: role ambiguity, demanding obligations, no input into decision-making, inadequate resources, understaffing, and extended hours.

Psychological dangers: work/family conflict, mental health risks, physical health risks, stress, and burnout.

Any practices contrary to working together as partners leaves us all vulnerable. Research has shown that up to 53 percent of employees are not engaged with their work at all and 17 percent are actively disengaged at work. This level of disengagement behind the wall leaves many opportunities for the offender population to divide and manipulate, which could be deadly. Disengagement also drives high staff turnover which tilts against experience, solidifying the stage for offender manipulation.

Unfortunately, the research also shows that managers account for 70 percent of the variance in employee engagement. It would be prudent for us as a system to revamp some of the management training so that they are better equipped to be more inclusive and effectively manage the talent pool.

The key message here is to remember that organizations with highly engaged employees see 59 percent less turnover. Engaged employees show up to work and stay, they find purpose in their work and are more committed to it. Teams that work well together are more committed to each other and their mutual goals, even beyond the organization.

We tackle contraband and the expectation that civilians do their part to keep the facility safe as they are not exempt from the consequences of complacency or deliberate indifference. Contraband is important because those are items that are illegal to possess behind the wall. They are any article or thing which a person confined in a detention facility is prohibited from obtaining or possessing by statute, rule, or order. See, contraband allows offenders to gain power over others and can effectively destabilize the security of an institution.

The last two modules of the training academy specifically deal with the development of soft skills and the importance of work/life balance. The word soft and Corrections are almost never used in the same sentence. Soft skills are human skills. Civilians need those most because all they have are their human skills when they are meeting with the population. It is the one thing that keeps us safe. We are not given mace or tasers or anything that could possibly protect us or serve as a deterrent to an attack. It is our soft skills that make some of us adept negotiators.

Work /life balance can seem impossible with mandatory overtime and, for many civilians, being on-call. We must constantly juggle conflicting demands, challenges of our roles, demanding relationships, frequent changes with little support and no input. As civilians, we are working in an environment where we are not trusted, for no reason, I must add; it's just the culture of the environment. In many places, we are seen as the enemy because we are the advocate.

The work of a service provider requires professionals to open our hearts and minds to the offenders (our patients). This very process of empathy is what makes us vulnerable to being profoundly affected and, dare I say, profoundly damaged by our work. Through training, we emphasize the importance of developing and maintaining strong social support and stress resiliency skills. We provide participants with tips to proactively mitigate the stress of the job.

I could no longer walk in fear. Every adverse experience I had brought me to this point. I was at a point in my life where I was strong enough, aware enough, had learned enough, and was confident that my voice was big enough to make a difference. ***VICTORY!***

Are you still thinking that you are not ready? Let's review the steps one more time:

1. Adjust **your** depth of focus

2. Create the mental distance **you** need to think and reflect

3. Tap into the social intelligence **you've** developed

4. Create a plan that leverages **your** practical intelligence and the new ways **you've** learned to solve problems

Chapter 9

The Entrepreneurial Cage: The Business of Things

"Be passionate about your life. Learn to live without fear of failing. Take a chance, you just might surprise yourself."

— Nishan Panwar

Ok, so let's not jump down my throat. The entrepreneurial road is an honorable one, but the reality is that you are responsible for the success of your business, so the grind never ends. You have many sleepless nights strategizing and repositioning. It is not a life for everyone. I've talked to many people who feel so free in their entrepreneurial space, just know that it took time and takes time to get there.

Being an entrepreneur can take you away from the people and activities you love most. **You are responsible for the success of your business.**

For me, I spent weeks researching and developing content. I am investing time now writing this book.

Some struggle to separate themselves from their entrepreneurial ventures and don't realize how much life they've missed. I am guilty. How about you? Some have mastered this work/life balance thing as it relates to being an entrepreneur, others continue to seek out ways to better manage their time, goals, and ambitions.

Well, I decided I would poll my Corrections network to garner social proof of concept. *VICTORY!*

I told them: This is what I'm thinking and here's what I'm going to do…

I got mixed reviews about it. Some could care less; they had already been burnt by the system and were just biding their time to retire. Others were skeptical and thought that it wouldn't be received well by Custody because it was created by an "outsider." Then there was that bunch that could not stop talking about how this was a great idea and they could not wait to see my training in their respective systems. Those were the ones who gave me constructive feedback and encouraged me to push forward. I am thankful to all who gave me their time and their feedback.

While I felt as though at that point I had done so much work, the reality was that the work was just beginning. I had a viable product, but I needed to do a Five Forces analysis on my offering. It took me some time to complete the analysis, but I got it done. *VICTORY!*

Next, I worked on a business plan. *VICTORY!* I had most of the information I needed to get started, and I figured that along the way, the offering would evolve, and a pricing structure would magically appear. Suffice it to say, that did not happen. I had to do much more research to get to a pricing model that made sense for the industry.

The biggest challenge I faced was that there was no other non-uniformed Corrections academy to benchmark. I used all different reports to come up with a model that made the most sense. I looked at the education sector and the trade school sector. I then researched the costs for training in the industry to ensure I was not going to price myself out of the market.

I decided to take a crack at the business model canvas because it would capture the key elements that should be included in a full business plan. In my mind, if I couldn't get this done, I certainly could not move forward. Turns out, I had done enough research to really give the process a go.

But wait, I needed to establish myself as a business and I really was not sure how to do that. So, more research to follow. What would I name the business? How would it be structured? Based on the pricing structure and projected profits, is there a legal structure better suited to handle the tax implications?

Lord, help me!

I was so far out of my depth, I just figured it best to quit now. But I did not. I pushed through the research and decided that an LLC would be appropriate to start and when the business truly takes off, we can

always seek to transition to a more appropriate structure. Once the LLC was formed, Alleyne & Co LLC
was official. ***VICTORY!***

From the Secretary of the state of Connecticut, I received a Certificate of Organization, Limited Liability
Company-Domestic. Following this, I registered with
the Department of Revenue Services and received my
Sales and Use Tax Permit. I went to the Department
of the Treasury for the Employer Identification Number. Days later, I received an email with my Articles
of Organization. I applied with the Department of
Administrative Services to be certified as a member
of the Supplier Diversity Program; certifying me as
a Black American Woman Owned Small/Minority
Business Enterprise. Months later, I would learn about
the System for Award Management, allowing me to do
business with the Federal government. ***VICTORY!***

Every victory served as a bit of encouragement and
motivation to keep moving forward. You must acknowledge all of the challenges that you have hurdled.

Those hurdles helped to build your muscles, helped
you to be stronger and jump higher.

I would recommend that anyone starting their journey, be patient with themselves. It is a lot to read
through and any errors will cause a delay in process-
ing, so take your time. If you need help, Alleyne & Co.
LLC provides professional coaching and mentoring to
correctional staffers.

I forgot to mention, if you are not doing business as

the official business name, you do need to file for a Certificate of Trade Name. As of October 22, 2019, I was officially doing business as the Civilian Corrections Academy.

Let the fun begin!

I didn't realize how creative I was until this journey began. Here I was creating social media posts, marketing materials, my own email campaigns, and creating my own logo. Well, with the logo, I paid for someone to create one and they didn't deliver what I was looking for, so I ended up teaching myself how to create logos. I even researched fonts to learn what the appropriate fonts were for my corporate audience.

I went from no social media presence to having a website: **www.ConnieAlleyne.com** (which I created myself). *VICTORY!* I developed a presence on Instagram, Facebook, Facebook Business, Twitter, LinkedIn, and Speaker Hub.

Just remember: the grind is real. I spent many sleepless nights milling over my business plan and my website.

Who knew?

Bring in: Fear.

All that hard work to get the product and the platforms ready for human consumption and fear had me paralyzed.

What if people do not like it? What if I'm sending

the wrong message? What if the messaging isn't consistent? What if no one is interested in my offering? Maybe I should change the colors? Is the wording right in the brochure?

You name it, I second-guessed it. One day I was talking to my good friend Sarah from business school, and she said, "Babe, your website is amazing, publish it! Your brochure is on point, send it out! What's the worst that could happen, Con?" It felt good to hear those reassuring words, but I was still afraid of the world rejecting me and everyone knowing I created something that was a flop.

Finally, I said, "God, I am doing your work. I am serving your people. Use me. Direct me. And if this is not your will, show me what you would have me do." I had to leave that on the altar for a few days, before, finally, I hit publish. And just like that my website and profiles were public.

I started engaging people on LinkedIn as the Founder and President of the Civilian Corrections Academy. In that first week of engagement, I was contacted by the Assistant Commissioner of a system, wanting to know more, and wanting to know how the training could make it to his system. He had 3500 civilians in his system. I was elated! In that same week, I was contacted by the President of the International Council of Women in Law Enforcement to speak at her law enforcement summit.

OMG?!?! Is this for real?

Could it be? Had I created something that the people wanted? That the people needed? Did I create a market or discover an untapped market? I'm still working that out for myself. I received a warmer welcome to the industry than anticipated.

I'm excited right now. Let me show you God's work one more time... I went and spoke at the summit and it turned out that I had the Dean of the School of Criminal Justice of Monroe College in my audience. She asked if we could speak following the summit and gave me her business card. Now, I did not know what could become of my curriculum in the world of academia. I did not create it for that audience, so the option was not in my purview. But God ... He arranged it so that not only would I be in talks with the dean, but we would discuss a teaching opportunity. Would you believe that I, me, would be teaching at Monroe College, the second largest criminal program in New York State? I would have the opportunity to train the next generation of civilians in Corrections. Adjunct Criminal Justice Professor has now been added to my resume!

All I can say is, "Only God." If we trust in Him, He will fulfill the promises He has for our lives.

My work was not done. I needed to have a solid marketing and promotions strategy: I needed to hire a salesperson and a researcher to help me. Remember, I am still working full-time at my day job and just like most entrepreneurs, I still had bills to pay and a child to provide for. Capitalization was my next step. How was I going to fund this venture?

It was great that I had been received well by the industry, but the lender lens is very different. I know that most lenders tend to look at businesses from a traditional lens and if they are not progressive in thought they will not be able to see the viability of the business.

As I suspected, I reached out to Key Bank only for the rep to give me a song and dance. I took what he told me and went back to my business plan to make some tweaks. Before going to another bank, I had done some research and found that in Connecticut there was a dedicated Small Business Development Center (please note that they are not only in Connecticut). However, I connected to an amazing Small Business Development Advisor here named Sade Owoye. She knew her stuff! We went through the business plan, she called in other resources for guidance on government matters and she never let me feel defeated. She told me I had a great business plan and that she had a tool that could take all of my inputs and create my financials. ***VICTORY!***

This was just what I needed!

To this day, I still reach out to her for guidance and she checks in to see how things are going and if there is anything I might need. I was able to take my business plan to the bank and secure my very first business line of credit.

All of this was happening when I meet Gary Cornelius on LinkedIn. Gary has a great book, *The Art of the Con*, which gives you good insight into the offender population. He had a solid history in Corrections and wanted to know more about Civilian Corrections Academy. After speaking, he offered to be of support if/when I needed it. He also told me of this guy in the industry who I might be interested in connecting to; his name was Anthony Gangi. Anthony is a correctional professional with almost two decades in the field and the host of a podcast called Tier Talk.

I called Anthony Gangi and he went right into interview mode. He's asking me questions and I'm answering them without hesitation. Did I mention that he happened to be the Superintendent for the New Jersey Department of Corrections? Little did I know, my chance encounter would lead to such an invaluable partnership.

I started out with one video, then two, now I've lost count. On his Tier Talk YouTube venue, we have covered so many topics and continue to pioneer solutions that influence the industry's conversation. I have had civilians and officers reach out to me to take training. We personally respond to his viewers, sharing our insights and hopefully helping them successfully navigate the issues that they face in the facility. Anthony continues to serve as a Corrections champion and advocate for officers and civilians.

In less than six months, I had the industry embrace me, the academic community embraced me, and was featured as a panel expert on a reputable industry platform.

One other thing, I was nominated to sit on the Board

of Trustees for M.A.S.C.A. (Middle Atlantic States Correctional Association). Me? Sitting on a Board of Trustees? Was I receiving validation that I had something of value to offer? MASCA is a non-profit organization comprised of members from CT, DE, MD, NJ, PA, NY, and DC. It is a professional organization for those involved in court administration, juvenile justice, probation and parole, institutional and community corrections, as well as for citizens with a vital interest in the juvenile and criminal justice fields.

Things were working in my favor and I could not be more grateful. I just wanted to take my business to the next level, and I did not know what that would require. I'm one of those people who does not sit on things for too long. Though I do believe there is a time to be still, I do not believe in wasting time. I decided I would work with a marketing team. I did not know what to expect, so I would lean on my common sense and the insights I had since acquired.

I had been pretty frugal all the while, but now I would be investing in the growth of the business; clearly, it had potential and I wanted to do this right. From December 2018 to July 2020, I had done all of my own marketing and promotions. All I could do is hope for the best and not hesitate to move on if we are not a good fit.

Fast forward a bit to the onset of COVID-19 in March of 2020, and Civilian Corrections Academy has now been recorded and made available on the teachable. com platform.

You might wonder why I'd do that.

Well, it is because I had several on-site events planned and now travel was banned, and events were being canceled. Was I supposed to wait before I pivoted? I could not afford to. Teachable.com was simple; I could build the courses myself and design my online school however I saw fit. The site gives students various payment options and allows me to monitor everything happening on the back end.

I'm so glad I added this web-based component. While folks in Corrections could not necessarily work from home, many facilities were now locked down and movement was only essential, so some staff were not as busy. They were looking for alternative ways to earn CEUs—Continuing Education Units. The same applied for those who were remote and looking for relevant learning opportunities.

If I were slow to identify the shift in the market and slow to adjust my business, I could become irrelevant quickly. Thankfully, that was not my fate. I continue to serve as a resource to my Corrections audience and serve as a resource to my students at Monroe College. Civilian Corrections Academy is slowly growing but I can feel movement with some powerful partnerships on the horizon.

Conclusion

Chapter 10

Constantine J. Alleyne

Being blessed would be a gross understatement of my life. Despite a few hiccups along the way, I was able to relocate to Connecticut and purchase a home to ensure that my daughter would grow up in a stable environment. I did my best to make sure she had a relationship with her dad, but he couldn't meet us halfway.

Yes, I was disappointed with the outcome, but I refused to let that hold me back. I had many moments when I thought I was not going to achieve my goals but having my family and friends there to encourage me made all the difference. I can't thank them enough. They always show up.

One day, I was in my bathroom crying my eyes out. Why? Because I thought maybe I made a wrong decision by leaving my hometown, Brooklyn, New York and my daughter's father. In walks my eighteen-month old, like little ones do, and gives me a hug. She didn't know what was wrong with Mommy, she just knew that she had never seen Mommy cry before, and it made her feel sad. All I could do in that moment was hug her back. I apologized to her if I had made the wrong decision but promised her that Mommy would do her best to make sure we had a happy life.

I've had to figure out how to make life happen for us. My support system is the best. They were here for us while I went to school for the EMBA, they continued to support me as I worked on my Advanced Business Certificate in Human Resource Management, and then again as I worked to complete my Diversity and Inclusion Certificate from Cornell University. They were there while I was locked in the office re-recording and editing the training for the online academy. I intentionally positioned myself in a manner that gives me multiple nets to safely fall into because I am responsible for protecting us.

My daughter, she's a trooper. I could not ask for a more understanding and supportive child. She has an old soul. She'll watch me study, record podcasts, cook her breakfast, lunch, and dinner. By the end of the night, she'll say, "Mommy, let's hug up." As much as I wish she would go get in her bed, it's just what I need. She is the reminder of why I work hard. She is the motivation to continue to press on because the quality of her life depends on her mom being able to make things happen.

Let's not get it twisted, before the COVID pandemic, this young lady had a social calendar of her own. As Mom, I was the chauffeur. She enjoys time with her cousins and friends, soccer, gymnastics, swimming, the running club, and the cooking club. Being her mom is **the** most important role in my life. During the pandemic I've also learned to embrace other roles that I did not know I would love, like entrepreneur, author, and founder. In many ways this pandemic was a gift and a curse, affording me the opportunity to slow down and get to know myself. It also allowed me to put some distance between me and my Cage of Comfort. **I AM FREE!**

Getting to know oneself is key to understanding your very own limits. Knowing your limits will guide how long you stay in any cage experience you may be in.

Sitting in the Cage of Comfort is easy because you created it. But navigating your Familial Cage may present to be much more difficult than you think as your family may play a significant role in your Cage of Comfort. Without dealing with your Familial Cage, you may struggle with your Cage of Safety because family may be where you feel the safest. As you draw on the strengths you've gained to conquer your personal cages, you will be better equipped to manage your Professional Cage.

As I consider the cage being a cocoon, I am brought to the thought of a batting cage.

Getting to know oneself is key to understanding your very own limits. Knowing your limits will guide how long you stay in any cage experience you may be in.

What is the purpose of a batting cage? I'm glad you asked.

A batting cage is where one goes to train and become proficient at baseball. This life we are living is similar to that batting cage. We are thrown many curve balls that teach us when to swing, when not to swing, how to be more efficient at living, how to make better decisions, and it teaches us to better discern what is best for our lives. I liken every cage experience to another round of practice in the batting cage. When we finally step out of that cage, we know we are better for it and when we play, oh, what a beautiful life we have made for ourselves.

We cannot fool ourselves into thinking that we are going to just decide and, poof, the cage will be gone. It simply does not work like that. Here's my challenge to you:

1. Adjust **your** depth of focus to one that matters most to **you**

2. Create the mental distance **you** need to think and reflect

3. Tap into the social intelligence that **you** have developed over the years

4. Create a plan that leverages **your** practical intelligence and the new ways that **you** have learned to solve problems

There comes a time where **you** must emerge and unleash your world changing capability, too. As Maya Angelou once said, "We delight in the beauty of the butterfly, but rarely admit the changes it has gone through to achieve that beauty."

When life gets really difficult, I challenge you to remember that you are transforming. While you are letting go of the past, be willing to welcome the new and give light to the whole new world you've created.

Nothing on my journey has been easy. I'm constantly learning something new. All things seem to prepare me for the next phase in my life, teaching me to turn my wounds into the wisdom that would inform my next steps. When folks start to complain about their lives, I just sit back and listen because I have seen depravity at its worst.

In all of the experiences I have had, I could identify with the struggle. Sheryl Sandberg said it best, "Each of us is more than the worst thing we've ever done." Behind the wall, you have individuals struggling with their life circumstances, some able to hurdle them and others not so much. Then you compound their loss of freedom with mental illness, lack of education, and other social ills that plague our communities. In the corporate world, I see my colleagues struggling to be the shiniest coin in the bunch. As an organization, I appreciate the focused efforts to level the playing field but there are but so many slots at the top. How far am I willing to go, and would I be willing to step on others to get there? It simply is not a race I want to run indefinitely.

Over the years, I've held on to my vision of excellence and dreams of success. I have constantly been on the hunt for who I have not yet become. I have passively absorbed the culture and political games that were being played, developed a practical intelligence and new ways of solving problems.

I can confidently say that I am becoming.

I had to lose my fear of things that I thought were impossible. My ability to detach and learn from my experiences continues to serve me well. Everything I worked to develop over the years has been to guide civilians away from common mistakes, keep them safe, and support their desire for a successful career in the world of Corrections.

Civilian Corrections Academy is my way of not just serving others but serving myself a hefty dose of self-compassion. It feels genuinely good to be utilizing all my gifts for me and my family. Any sleep deprivation I might experience is because I am working on my labor of love and fulfilling my dreams, no one else's.

I will close here by saying this: Once you come to terms with the fact that there is no shortcut to excellence, it makes the good and the bad of your life's journey more palatable.

So, make each day a masterpiece!

How much longer will you allow yourself to remain a caterpillar?

"The battles that count aren't the ones for gold medals. The struggles within yourself—the invisible, inevitable battles inside all of us—that's where it's at."

— JESSE OWENS

ACKNOWLEDGMENTS

As with most of the things that I accomplished in my life this book would not have been possible without God and the love and support of my family and friends.

Though I have been blessed to have the unconditional love and support of both of my parents, I must shout out to my mom who intentionally built my self-esteem. From the time I could remember, she told me that I was smart, I was beautiful, I was strong, I was loved, and most importantly, I was a child of God. Because of her, I moved through my world with an unequivocal confidence in knowing that I was enough. Her continuous reinforcement empowered me to confidently navigate any adversity that I faced. To this day, she reminds me that there is nothing I cannot do once I put my mind to something.

There is a host whose insight, perspective, championship, and encouragement have mattered. Thanks to Aneka, Roshawn, and LaQueta for your friendships, encouragement and support from high school, undergrad, through now. To my grandmother Glendora Castello. Your life and passing solidified my desire to serve vulnerable populations.

Tiffany Donelson, President and CEO at Connecticut Health Foundation and I were having a conversation about me considering the UCONN EMBA and she confirmed that there was no decision to be made. Her words were, "There's never really a good time to go back to school and what better example could you set for your daughter?" As insignificant as that conversation may have seemed in the moment, it was the mark of a pivotal moment in time.

My girls, StacyAnn Walker and Desiree Jacobs, are not only friends and confidants to me but aunties to Kendall. They cared for Kendall while I went through school commitments when my mom and brother John could not make it to Connecticut. That kind of support is invaluable, and I will forever be grateful for having them in my corner cheering me on.

I am full of gratitude for my 2017 EMBA cohort. Sarah Macary became my sister from another mother and Luis Arzu became my brother from another mother. We identified each other's strengths and served as each other's anchors. The degree content was challenging but we would not leave each other behind.

Creative stimulation includes Anthony Gangi and Geovanni Derice. Though we met Anthony by chance our connection to the world of Corrections is undeniable. We have partnered on many ventures and will continue to collaborate to bridge the gap that exists between civilians and custodial staff, a shared passion. Geovanni, my "Book Doula" guided me through the process of amplifying my voice and effectively allowing readers to see my spirituality while accessing my intellect. His crisp ability to encourage independent thought and creativity is very much appreciated.

Last but certainly not least, my baby girl, Kendall Wyche. I have no words to express my heart and love for this kind and thoughtful girl. Over the years, Kendall has given me the time and space to study and to write. While she may have her moments when she just wants Mommy time, it is in those moments that I realize what an amazing little girl I've been blessed with. She has taught me to balance the drive to succeed with self-care. All that I do is to make sure she knows she is loved. She has a mommy that will work her fingers to the bone to ensure a happy and stable childhood. I do not do that alone. By now you can see that I could not do any of this without the support of my family and friends. They are a blessing to me that I do not take for granted. They may not know this but they help me to always be my authentic self. Thank you.

ABOUT THE AUTHOR

Prior to trailblazing her path and establishing Alleyne & Co., Constantine Alleyne was a Health Services Manager on Rikers Island and served as Health Services Administrator II for the Connecticut Department of Corrections. Her tenure spans almost two decades of correctional and human resource management experience, holding a Master's in Public Health from Long Island University; an Executive Masters in Business Administration and an Advanced Business Certificate in Human Resource Management from the University of Connecticut; and a Diversity and Inclusion Certificate from Cornell University.

Throughout Constantine's correctional career she has proven herself to be a collaborative leader who forges strong relationships to effectively foster an environment of trust, respect, and opportunity for civilian employees. She has been able to partner with Custody leaderships at all levels. She understands the complexity of the institution's employees and population dynamics and has successfully led a number of small and large teams, leveraging the collective intelligence to make more informed decisions.

Constantine decided to diversify— taking on a role in the aerospace industry but quickly discovered that although her skills were transferable her heart was in Corrections. In 2018, Constantine established Civilian Corrections Academy, a subsidiary of Alleyne & Co LLC. She is an Adjunct Criminal Justice Professor at Monroe College, training the next generation of civilian employees seeking to enter some aspect of Law Enforcement. Today, she proudly sits on the Middle Atlantic States Correctional Association (M.A.S.C.A.) Board of Trustees while continuously monitoring the correctional landscape and positioning herself to better serve the industry.

Made in the USA
Middletown, DE
07 September 2024

59915471R00097